Tiziana Lo Porto and Daniele Marotta
Superzelda: The Graphic Life of Zelda Fitzgerald

Copyright © 2011 by minimum fax
Translation copyright © 2013 by One Peace Books

All rights reserved.

Originally published in 2011 by minimum fax, Italy, as *Superzelda: La vita disegnata di Zelda Fitzgerald*

First edition published by One Peace Books, 2013
1 2 3 4 5 6 7 8 9 10

Translation by Antony Shugaar
Design by Daniele Marotta

ISBN: 978-1-935548-27-0

Printed in Canada

Distributed by SCB Distributors
www.scbdistributors.com

For more information, contact:
One Peace Books
43-32 22nd Street, #204
Long Island City, NY 11101
www.onepeacebooks.com

Fonts:
Danimarot (Daniele Marotta, 2011), interior
ITC Rennie Mackintosh (Rennie Mackintosh and Phil Grimshaw, 1996), cover

TIZIANA LO PORTO
DANIELE MAROTTA

———

SUPERZELDA
THE GRAPHIC LIFE OF ZELDA FITZGERALD

TRANSLATED FROM THE ITALIAN BY ANTONY SHUGAAR

ONE PEACE
BOOKS

CONTENTS

NOW THE TIME HAS COME FOR HER REAPPRAISAL, A NEW APPRECIATION THAT WE HAIL WITH JOY BECAUSE WE HAVE ALWAYS FOUND HER ENORMOUSLY SYMPATHETIC DESERVING OF COMPREHENSION, JUDGING FROM THE PHOTOGRAPHS THAT CIRCULATE, AND FROM THE MEMORABLE DEEDS AND PHRASES ATTRIBUTED TO HER; INDEED, WE HAVE ALWAYS BEEN JUST AS SUSPICIOUS OF THE INFERNAL LEGENDS THAT SURROUND HER, EVERY BIT AS MUCH AS WE ARE OF THE GOLDEN LEGEND THAT ATTACHES TO HIM.

ATTILIO BERTOLUCCI, "ZELDA AND SCOTT"

AND IN AN HUNDRED YEARS I THINK I SHALL LIKE HAVING YOUNG PEOPLE SPECULATE ON WHETHER MY EYES WERE BROWN OR BLUE—OF COURSE, THEY ARE NEITHER.

ZELDA IN A LETTER TO SCOTT, 1919

PROLOGUE

FAMILY PHOTO ALBUM

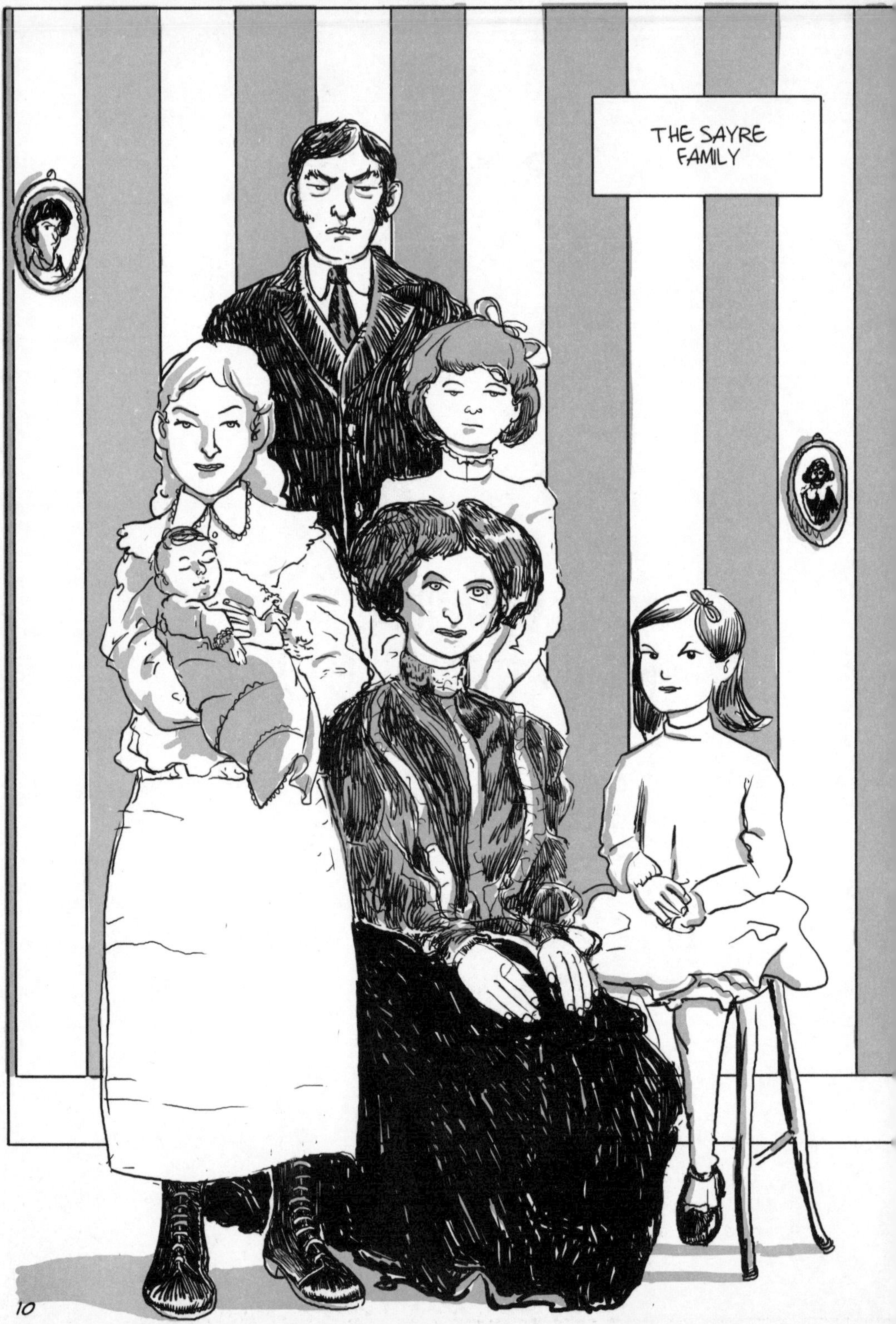
THE SAYRE FAMILY

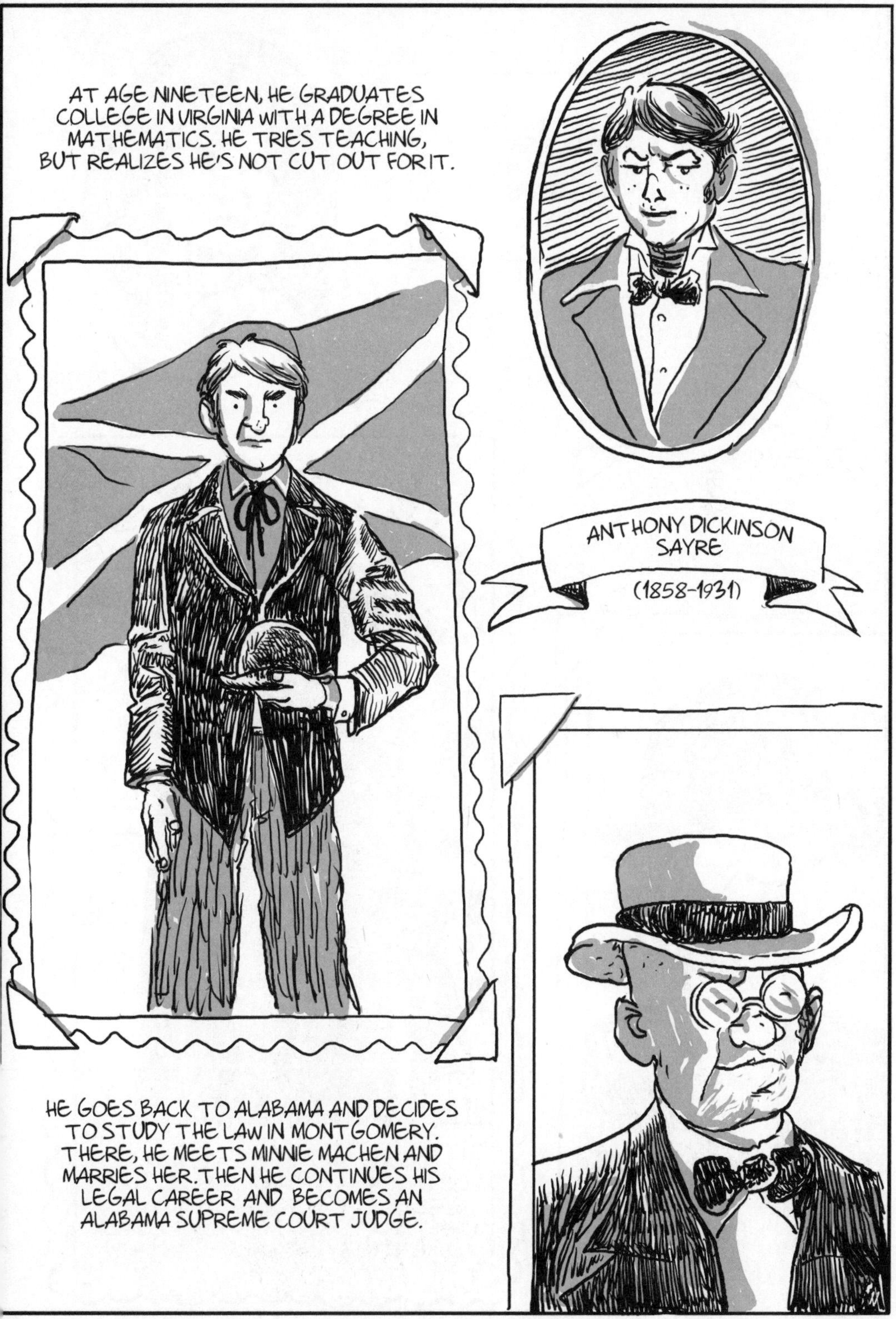
AT AGE NINETEEN, HE GRADUATES COLLEGE IN VIRGINIA WITH A DEGREE IN MATHEMATICS. HE TRIES TEACHING, BUT REALIZES HE'S NOT CUT OUT FOR IT.
ANTHONY DICKINSON SAYRE
(1858-1931)
HE GOES BACK TO ALABAMA AND DECIDES TO STUDY THE LAW IN MONTGOMERY. THERE, HE MEETS MINNIE MACHEN AND MARRIES HER. THEN HE CONTINUES HIS LEGAL CAREER AND BECOMES AN ALABAMA SUPREME COURT JUDGE.

SHE'S THE ARTIST OF THE FAMILY. HER FATHER SENDS HER TO MISS CHILTON'S FINISHING SCHOOL IN MONTGOMERY.

MINNIE MACHEN

(1860-1958)

THERE, SHE MEETS ANTHONY DICKINSON SAYRE AND LAUNCHES HER CAREER IN THE THEATER. BUT HER FAMILY IS OPPOSED, SO SHE GOES BACK TO KENTUCKY AND MARRIES ANTHONY.

MARJORIE SAYRE

THE ELDEST OF THE SAYRE SISTERS. SHE IS ALSO THE SICKLIEST. SHE BECOMES A SCHOOLMISTRESS AND SPENDS THE REST OF HER LIFE BATTLING NERVOUS EXHAUSTION.

13

THE SECOND-BORN SAYRE DAUGHTER. SHE IS THE SMARTEST OF THE SAYRE SISTERS.

ROSALIND SAYRE

SHE TAKES A JOB AT THE FIRST NATIONAL BANK, MAKING HER THE FIRST GIRL IN MONTGOMERY TO WORK AS ANYTHING OTHER THAN A SCHOOL TEACHER.

CLOTILDE SAYRE

THE PRETTIEST SISTER,
AND ALSO THE ONE WHOM ZELDA
FIGHTS WITH MOST OFTEN.

15

ANTHONY D. SAYRE, JR.

HE QUITS HIS STUDIES, ANNOUNCING THAT THERE IS NOTHING HE WOULD RATHER DO THAN PAINT. BUT THEN HE DOESN'T. IN 1933, HE COMMITS SUICIDE.

1.

A CHILD OF THE TWENTIETH CENTURY

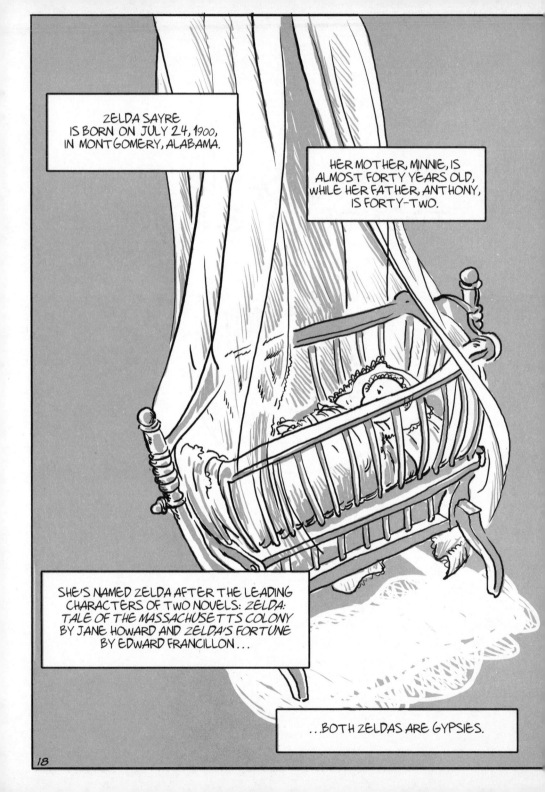

ZELDA SAYRE IS BORN ON JULY 24, 1900, IN MONTGOMERY, ALABAMA.

HER MOTHER, MINNIE, IS ALMOST FORTY YEARS OLD, WHILE HER FATHER, ANTHONY, IS FORTY-TWO.

SHE'S NAMED ZELDA AFTER THE LEADING CHARACTERS OF TWO NOVELS: *ZELDA: TALE OF THE MASSACHUSETTS COLONY* BY JANE HOWARD AND *ZELDA'S FORTUNE* BY EDWARD FRANCILLON...

...BOTH ZELDAS ARE GYPSIES.

18

TELL ME ABOUT MYSELF WHEN I WAS LITTLE.

YOU WERE A GOOD BABY.

AND DID I CRY AT NIGHT AND RAISE HELL SO YOU AND DADDY WISHED I WAS DEAD?

WHAT AN IDEA! ALL MY CHILDREN WERE SWEET CHILDREN!

AND GRANDMA'S, TOO?

I SUPPOSE SO.

YOUR GRANDMOTHER WAS A QUEER OLD LADY.

THEN WHY DID SHE RUN UNCLE CAL AWAY WHEN HE CAME HOME FROM THE CIVIL WAR?

CAL, TOO?

YES. WHEN CAL CAME HOME, GRANDMA SENT WORD TO FLORENCE FEATHER THAT IF SHE WAS WAITING FOR HER TO DIE TO MARRY CAL, SHE WANTED THE FEATHERS TO KNOW THAT THE SAYRE WERE A LONG-LIVED RACE.

SO CAL DIDN'T MARRY, AFTER ALL?

NO— GRAND- MOTHERS ALWAYS HAVE THEIR WAY.

IF I'D BEEN UNCLE CAL, I WOULDN'T HAVE STOOD IT. I'D HAVE DONE WHAT I WANTED TO DO.

19

I WAS A HYPERACTIVE, TIRELESS LITTLE GIRL. I WAS INDEPENDENT-MINDED, COURAGEOUS, AND INDIFFERENT TO ANYONE ELSE'S OPINION, EVEN IF I ALMOST ALWAYS PLAYED ON MY OWN.

ROBERTSON'S GOLDEN SHRED

WHAT A BORE BEING THE ONLY CHILD IN THE HOUSE.

NUMBER OF THE FIRE DEPARTMENT

HURRY, GENTLEMEN! THERE'S A LITTLE GIRL ON THE ROOF OF A HOUSE!

EEEEEEEEEEE

HELP! SAVE ME!

ZELDA FINDS WAYS TO AMUSE HERSELF.

21

AT AGE SIX, ZELDA STARTS SCHOOL, BUT SHE DOESN'T LIKE IT AND GOES HOME.

SHE TRIES AGAIN THE FOLLOWING YEAR.

MAMMAAA!

1913

BUT SHE STILL DOESN'T THINK MUCH OF SCHOOL.

MAMMA, I DON'T WANT TO GO TO SCHOOL ANYMORE.

WHY NOT?

I SEEM TO KNOW EVERYTHING.

23

IN HER FIRST YEAR OF HIGH SCHOOL, ZELDA GETS GOOD GRADES, HAS ALMOST PERFECT ATTENDANCE, AND EXCELS IN ENGLISH AND MATH.

A DOUBLE BANANA SPLIT.

AFTER SCHOOL, SHE'S GIVEN MORE FREEDOM THAN HER CLASSMATES...

...AND IN THE EVENING, WHEN SHE COMES HOME, SHE READS EVERY BOOK SHE CAN GET HER HANDS ON.

1914

24

SHE SECRETLY USES HER SISTERS' MAKEUP. IF SHE IS ACCUSED OF THIS POACHING, SHE FREELY DENIES THE OBVIOUS.

25

I WANT TO GO TO NEW YORK, MAMMA.

WHAT ON EARTH FOR?

TO BE MY OWN BOSS.

WELL...BEING BOSS ISN'T A QUESTION OF PLACES.

WHY CAN'T YOU BE BOSS AT HOME?

2.

FUNDAMENTAL ZELDA

A SOUTHERN MOON IS A SODDEN MOON, AND SULTRY.

WHILE SHE SLEEPS, ZELDA GROWS UP.

AT AGE SIXTEEN, ZELDA MAKES A SUCCESSFUL BALLET DEBUT AT THE OLD CITY AUDITORIUM.

BRAVA!!!

THE ADVERTISER

She has the straightest nose, the most determined little chin and the bluest eyes in Montgomery. She might dance like Pavlova if her nimble feet were not so busy keeping up with the pace a string of young but ardent admirers set for her.

VRROOOMM...

ZELDA!

EVEN THOUGH SHE LOVES TO DANCE, HER BURGEONING SOCIAL CALENDAR STARTS TO INTERFERE WITH HER LESSONS.

30

ZELDA IS SIMPLY FEARLESS. SHE'S NOT AFRAID OF BOYS, AND SHE'S NOT AFRAID OF BEING THE TARGET OF GOSSIP. SHE'S AFRAID OF ABSOLUTELY NOTHING.

THE DIVING BOARD IS SO HIGH, ALMOST NO ONE HAS THE COURAGE TO USE IT.

ZELDA DOES, AND, ONCE AGAIN, SHE VENTURES WHERE ALMOST EVERYONE ELSE FEARS TO FOLLOW.

SHE SAYS THE ONLY THINGS SHE CARES ABOUT ARE SWIMMING AND BOYS. RUMORS CIRCULATE THAT SHE GOES SKINNY DIPPING. SHE LAUGHS IT OFF, BUT DOES NOTHING TO DENY THE RUMORS.

WHAT ARE YOU THINKING ABOUT?

ABOUT FUN!

SHE IS AT SEVENTEEN A PHILOSOPHICAL GOURMAND OF POSSIBILITIES.

THERE'S GONNA BE A WAR!!

THEN THE DANCE OUGHT TO BE GOOD TONIGHT.

AND AS AMERICA READIES FOR WAR, THE DEBUTANTE SEASON BEGINS FOR ZELDA.

THE WAR BRINGS MEN TO THE TOWN LIKE SWARMS OF BENEVOLENT LOCUSTS...

...EATING AWAY THE BLIGHT OF UNMARRIED WOMEN THAT HAD OVERRUN THE SOUTH SINCE ITS ECONOMIC DECLINE.

33

HEY, ZELDA, LOOKIE HERE! ISN'T THAT ONE OF YOUR SUITORS?

WHY, SHOULDN'T HE HAVE GIVEN THAT PHOTO TO YOU?

BUT ZELDA'S NOT LIKE THE OTHER GIRLS...

STUDIO

YOUR CHOICE PHOTO

CRASH!

...INSTEAD OF WAITING, SHE TAKES WHAT SHE THINKS SHE DESERVES.

READING THE STORY OF ZELDA FITZGERALD... I IDENTIFIED WITH HER MUTINOUS SPIRIT. I REMEMBER PASSING SHOP WINDOWS WITH MY MOTHER AND ASKING WHY PEOPLE DIDN'T JUST KICK THEM IN.

PATTI SMITH

34

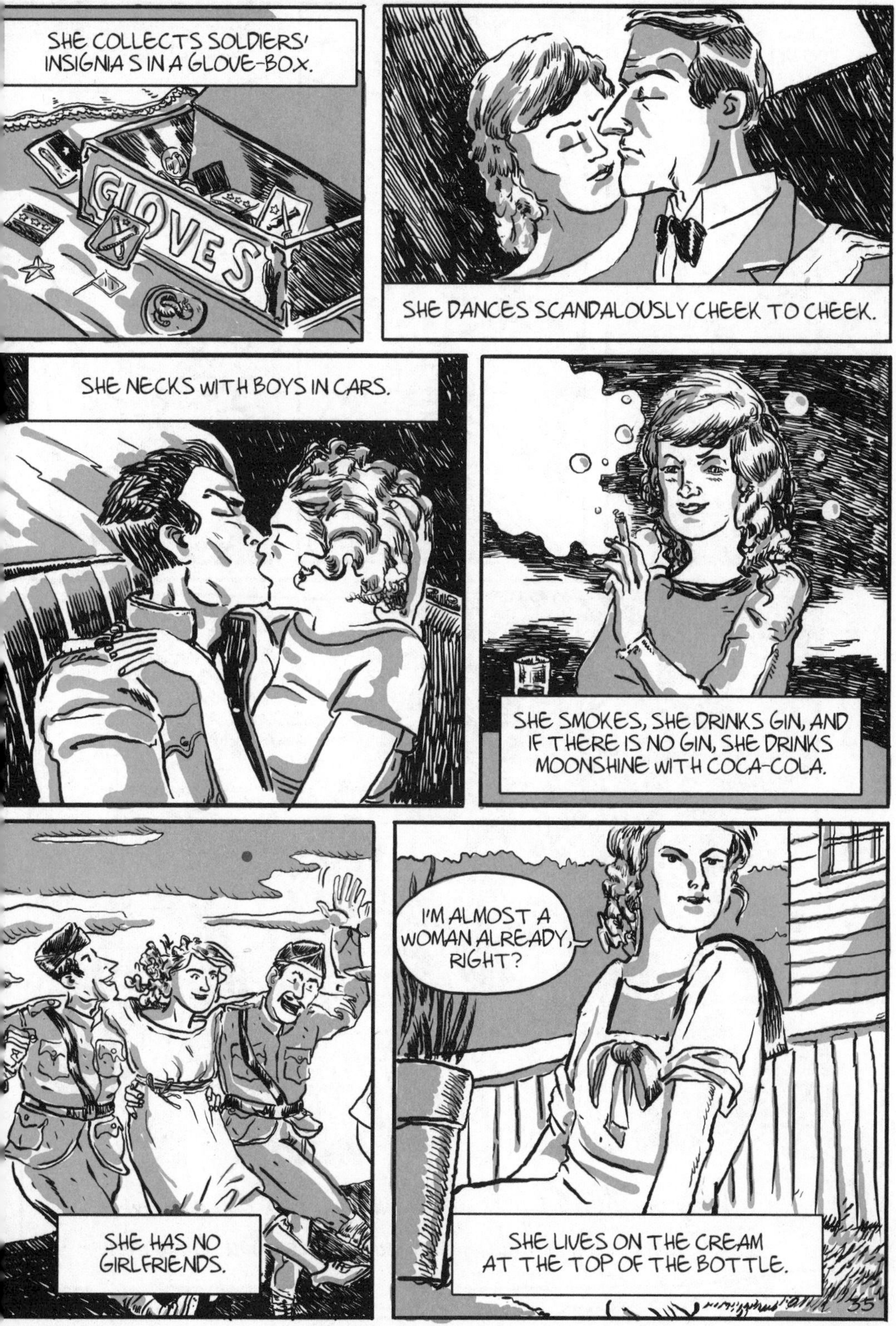
SHE COLLECTS SOLDIERS' INSIGNIA S IN A GLOVE-BOX.
GLOVES
SHE DANCES SCANDALOUSLY CHEEK TO CHEEK.
SHE NECKS WITH BOYS IN CARS.
SHE SMOKES, SHE DRINKS GIN, AND IF THERE IS NO GIN, SHE DRINKS MOONSHINE WITH COCA-COLA.
SHE HAS NO GIRLFRIENDS.
I'M ALMOST A WOMAN ALREADY, RIGHT?
SHE LIVES ON THE CREAM AT THE TOP OF THE BOTTLE.

THERE'S NOTHING TO DO BUT DRINK AND MAKE LOVE.

I'M PRETTY— AT LEAST THAT'S WHAT THEY TELL ME.

I'M THE MOST POPULAR GIRL IN HIGH SCHOOL.

ZELDA IS INDEED VOTED THE PRETTIEST AND THE MOST ATTRACTIVE GIRL IN HER CLASS. BUT BY GRADUATION, HER GRADES HAVE SLIPPED, AND HER CONDUCT IS DEEMED "UNSATISFACTORY." SHE AMUSES HERSELF BY WRITING POETRY...

Why should all life be work, when we all can borrow.
Let's think only of today, and not worry about tomorrow.

36

3.

SCOTT, MEET ZELDA

JULY 1918

LIEUTENANT FRANCIS SCOTT KEY FITZGERALD, IRISH CATHOLIC, BORN SEPTEMBER 24, 1896, IN ST. PAUL, MINNESOTA.

DO YOU WANT TO DANCE?

38

WE EVEN RESEMBLE EACH OTHER PHYSICALLY.

THERE SEEMED TO BE SOME HEAVENLY SUPPORT BENEATH HIS SHOULDER BLADES THAT LIFTED HIS FEET FROM THE GROUND... AS IF HE SECRETLY ENJOYED THE ABILITY TO FLY.

YOU HAVE THE SAME POINT OF VIEW ON MEN THAT I HAVE ON WOMEN.

I'M NOT REALLY FEMININE, YOU KNOW, IN MY MIND.

OH, I'M BRIGHT, QUITE SELFISH, EMOTIONAL WHEN AROUSED, FOND OF ADMIRATION—

I DON'T WANT TO FALL IN LOVE WITH YOU—

NOBODY ASKED YOU TO.

BUT I PROBABLY WILL. I LOVE YOUR MOUTH.

HUSH! PLEASE DON'T FALL IN LOVE WITH MY MOUTH. HAIR, EYES, SHOULDERS, SLIPPERS...

...BUT NOT MY MOUTH. EVERYBODY FALLS IN LOVE WITH MY MOUTH.

IT'S QUITE BEAUTIFUL.

IT'S TOO SMALL.

NO IT ISN'T—

LET'S SEE.

ZELDA FLIRTS WITH SCOTT...

SAY SOMETHING SWEET.

LORD HELP ME.

WELL, DON'T— IF IT'S SO HARD.

SHALL WE PRETEND? SO SOON?

LET'S PRETEND.

NO—I CAN'T— IT'S SENTIMENT.

YOU'RE NOT SENTIMENTAL?

NO, I'M ROMANTIC—A SENTIMENTAL PERSON THINKS THINGS WILL LAST—A ROMANTIC PERSON HOPES AGAINST HOPE THAT THEY WON'T. SENTIMENT IS EMOTIONAL.

AND YOU'RE NOT?

WELL— DON'T ARGUE— KISS ME AGAIN.

NO— I HAVE NO DESIRE TO KISS YOU.

...WHO FLIRTS WITH ZELDA...

YOU HAVEN'T KISSED ME FOR TWO WEEKS. I HAD AN IDEA THAT AFTER A GIRL WAS KISSED SHE WAS—WAS— WON.

THOSE DAYS ARE OVER.

I HAVE TO BE WON ALL OVER AGAIN EVERY TIME YOU SEE ME.

ARE YOU SERIOUS?

ABOUT AS USUAL. THERE USED TO BE TWO KINDS OF KISSES: FIRST WHEN GIRLS WERE KISSED AND DESERTED; SECOND, WHEN THEY WERE ENGAGED. NOW THERE'S A THIRD KIND, WHERE THE MAN IS KISSED AND DESERTED. IF MR. JONES OF THE NINETIES BRAGGED HE'D KISSED A GIRL, EVERY ONE KNEW HE WAS THROUGH WITH HER.

IF MR. JONES OF 1919 BRAGS THE SAME EVERY ONE KNOWS IT'S BECAUSE HE CAN'T KISS HER ANY MORE. GIVEN A DECENT START ANY GIRL CAN BEAT A MAN NOWADAYS.

...WHO FALLS IN LOVE WITH SCOTT...

41

SAY "DEAR."

YOU LOVE ME. WHY WON'T YOU?

NO.

WHY WON'T YOU TALK TO ME?

I NEVER SAY ANYTHING TO ANYBODY.

TELL ME YOU LOVE ME.

OH— I LOVE YOU. DO YOU LOVE ME?

AREN'T YOU INTERESTED IN ANYTHING EXCEPT YOURSELF?

GIN

NOT MUCH.

WHY, YOU'VE BOBBED YOUR HAIR!

YES, ISN'T IT GORGEOUS?

...WHO FALLS IN LOVE WITH ZELDA.

42

SO MUCH I LOVE THE MAN, SO CLOSE AND CLOSER I FEEL MYSELF THAT HE BECOMES DISTORTED IN MY VISION, LIKE PRESSING MY NOSE UPON A MIRROR AND GAZING INTO MY OWN EYES.

ZELDA IS—UTTERLY ZELDA. SHE IS ONE OF THOSE GIRLS WHO NEED NEVER MAKE THE SLIGHTEST EFFORT TO HAVE MEN FALL IN LOVE WITH THEM. TWO TYPES OF MEN SELDOM DO: DULL MEN ARE USUALLY AFRAID OF HER CLEVERNESS AND INTELLECTUAL MEN ARE USUALLY AFRAID OF HER BEAUTY. ALL OTHERS ARE HERS BY NATURAL PREROGATIVE.

43

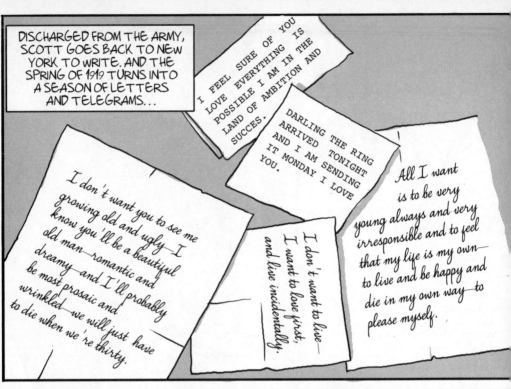

DISCHARGED FROM THE ARMY, SCOTT GOES BACK TO NEW YORK TO WRITE. AND THE SPRING OF 1919 TURNS INTO A SEASON OF LETTERS AND TELEGRAMS...

I FEEL SURE OF YOU LOVE EVERYTHING IS POSSIBLE I AM IN THE LAND OF AMBITION AND SUCCES.

DARLING THE RING ARRIVED TONIGHT AND I AM SENDING IT MONDAY I LOVE YOU.

I don't want you to see me growing old and ugly—I know you'll be a beautiful old man—romantic and dreamy—and I'll probably be most prosaic and wrinkled—we will just have to die when we're thirty.

I don't want to live—I want to love first, and live incidentally.

All I want is to be very young always and very irresponsible and to feel that my life is my own—to live and be happy and die in my own way—to please myself.

...AND GIFTS.

THESE PAJAMAS ARE THE MOST ADORABLY MOON-SHINY THING ON EARTH— I FEEL LIKE A VOGUE COVER IN 'EM...

...BUT I FEEL SURE I'LL NEVER BE ABLE TO KEEP OFF THE STREET IN 'EM.

44

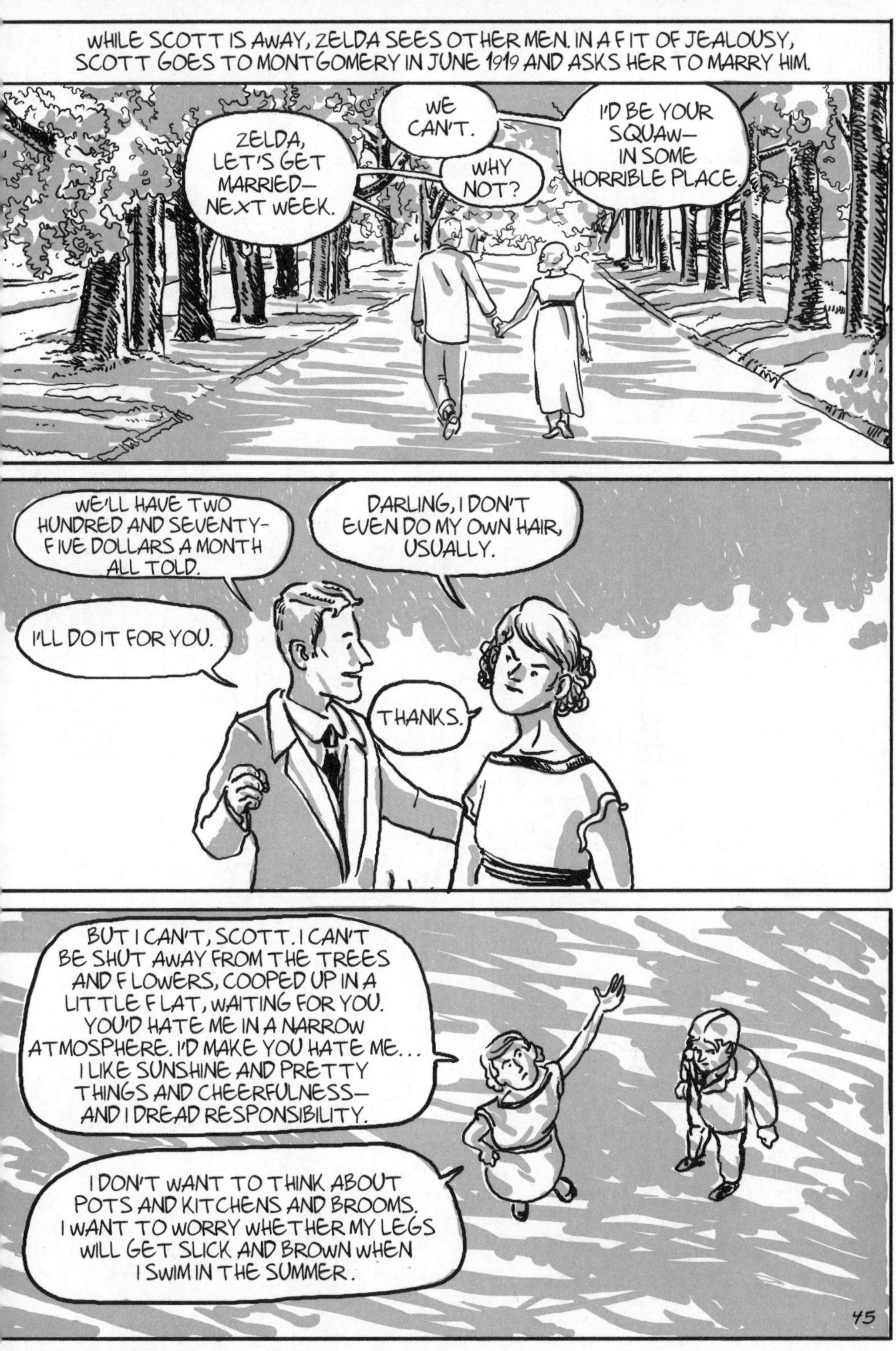
WHILE SCOTT IS AWAY, ZELDA SEES OTHER MEN. IN A FIT OF JEALOUSY, SCOTT GOES TO MONTGOMERY IN JUNE 1919 AND ASKS HER TO MARRY HIM.
ZELDA, LET'S GET MARRIED— NEXT WEEK.
WE CAN'T.
WHY NOT?
I'D BE YOUR SQUAW— IN SOME HORRIBLE PLACE.
WE'LL HAVE TWO HUNDRED AND SEVENTY-FIVE DOLLARS A MONTH ALL TOLD.
DARLING, I DON'T EVEN DO MY OWN HAIR, USUALLY.
I'LL DO IT FOR YOU.
THANKS.
BUT I CAN'T, SCOTT. I CAN'T BE SHUT AWAY FROM THE TREES AND FLOWERS, COOPED UP IN A LITTLE FLAT, WAITING FOR YOU. YOU'D HATE ME IN A NARROW ATMOSPHERE. I'D MAKE YOU HATE ME... I LIKE SUNSHINE AND PRETTY THINGS AND CHEERFULNESS— AND I DREAD RESPONSIBILITY.
I DON'T WANT TO THINK ABOUT POTS AND KITCHENS AND BROOMS. I WANT TO WORRY WHETHER MY LEGS WILL GET SLICK AND BROWN WHEN I SWIM IN THE SUMMER.

SCOTT AND ZELDA BREAK UP. WITH HIS MOTHER'S RING IN HIS POCKET, SCOTT GOES BACK TO NEW YORK...

...AND FROM THERE, TO ST. PAUL, WHERE HE SPENDS THE SUMMER REWRITING HIS NOVEL.

THE TWO SEE EACH OTHER IN THE FALL OF 1919, WHEN SCRIBNER'S DECIDES TO PUBLISH SCOTT'S NOVEL, AND HE MAKES UP HIS MIND TO WIN BACK ZELDA.

THE HEROINE DOES RESEMBLE YOU IN MORE WAYS THAN FOUR.

I AM VERY PROUD OF YOU... IT'S SO NICE TO KNOW THAT YOU REALLY CAN DO THINGS—ANYTHING—AND I LOVE TO FEEL THAT MAYBE I CAN HELP JUST A LITTLE.

ON MARCH 20, 1920, THE SAYRES OFFICIALLY ANNOUNCE THE ENGAGEMENT.

THIS SIDE OF PARADISE

ON MARCH 26, THIS SIDE OF PARADISE, BY FRANCIS SCOTT FITZGERALD, IS PUBLISHED. AND IT'S AN IMMEDIATE HIT.

4.

THE WEDDING

I WANT TO MARRY SCOTT, BECAUSE HUSBANDS ARE SO OFTEN "HUSBANDS" AND I MUST MARRY A LOVER.

THERE ARE FOUR GENERAL TYPES OF HUSBANDS.

THE HUSBAND WHO ALWAYS WANTS TO STAY IN IN THE EVENING, HAS NO VICES, AND WORKS FOR A SALARY. TOTALLY UNDESIRABLE!

THE ATAVISTIC MASTER WHOSE MISTRESS ONE IS, TO WAIT ON HIS PLEASURE. THIS SORT ALWAYS CONSIDERS EVERY PRETTY WOMAN "SHALLOW," A SORT OF PEACOCK WITH ARRESTED DEVELOPMENT.

NEXT COMES THE WORSHIPPER, THE IDOLATER OF HIS WIFE AND ALL THAT IS HIS, TO THE UTTER OBLIVION OF EVERYTHING ELSE. THIS SORT DEMANDS AN EMOTIONAL ACTRESS FOR A WIFE.

GOD! IT MUST BE AN EXERTION TO BE THOUGHT RIGHTEOUS.

AND SCOTT— A TEMPORARILY PASSIONATE LOVER WITH WISDOM ENOUGH TO REALIZE WHEN IT HAS FLOWN AND THAT IT MUST FLY. AND I WANT TO GET MARRIED TO HIM.

SCOTT AND ZELDA ARE MARRIED IN NEW YORK ON APRIL 3, 1920.

SMILE!

49

zelda

WOW.

2019

AND THEY SPEND THEIR WEDDING NIGHT AT THE BILTMORE HOTEL...

...OPENING GIFTS...

I DIDN'T THINK WHEN...

WHEN YOU RECEIVE THIS CARD, I'LL BE FAR AWAY...

I WISH YOU ALL THE BEST...

...DRINKING.

ANOTHER GIN RICKEY?

NEVER SAY ANOTHER. BAD MANNERS...GOOD WAITER NEVER RUBS A GUEST'S NOSE IN HIS OWN LACK 'O WILL POWER.

...PARTYING IN THEIR HOTEL SUITE.

WE CAN'T SLEEP IN HERE. EITHER YOU KICK THEM OUT, OR WE LEAVE!!!!

I'M TERRIBLY SORRY, MADAM, I'LL TAKE CARE OF IT.

IT'S THEM AGAIN, THE FITZGERALDS IN SUITE 2109. THEY'RE GOING TO HEAR FROM ME!!!

WHERE THE DEVIL HAVE THEY GOT TO?

OH... MY... WHAT'S THIS?!

THAT VERY NIGHT, THE FITZGERALDS ARE THROWN OUT OF THE BILTMORE HOTEL.

zelda

AFTER BEING KICKED OUT OF THE BILTMORE, THEY CHECK IN TO THE COMMODORE, NEARBY...

...RESUMING THEIR ECCENTRIC NEW YORK HONEYMOON...

...INDIFFERENT TO WHAT THE CITY MIGHT HAVE TO SAY ABOUT THEM.

WHAT THEY SAY ABOUT ZELDA...

SHE'S A TRAGI-CALLY BRILLIANT GIRL WHO HAS FAILED AS A SOCIAL CREATURE.

LOUISE BROOKS

THIS SIDE OF PARADISE

BUT THAT'S ME!

I'VE NEVER THOUGHT SHE'S BEAUTIFUL. SHE'S VERY BLOND WITH A CANDY BOX FACE AND A LITTLE BOW MOUTH, VERY MUCH ON THE SMALL SCALE AND THERE'S SOMETHING PETULANT ABOUT HER. IF SHE DOESN'T LIKE SOMETHING SHE SULKS; I DON'T FIND THAT AN ATTRACTIVE TRAIT.

DOROTHY PARKER

SHE CHEWS GUM AND SHOWS HER KNEES. BOTH ARE DRINKING HEAVILY. I THINK THEY WILL BE DIVORCED IN THREE YEARS

ALEXANDER MCKAIG

MOST PEOPLE NOWADAYS FEEL THAT MARRIAGE AND LIFE DON'T GO TOGETHER. BUT NOTHING DOES GO WITH LIFE.

IF I WERE A MAN I WOULDN'T GET MARRIED.

SHE PASSES VERY QUICKLY FROM ONE TOPIC TO ANOTHER.

LAWTON CAMPBELL

53

BUT SCOTT ADORES EVERYTHING ABOUT ZELDA.

I'LL BET YOU DON'T KNOW HALF WHAT YOU SHOULD ABOUT ZELDA.

WHY, SCOTT... I KNOW ALL THERE IS TO KNOW ABOUT ZELDA; I'M HER MOTHER.

WELL, YOU COULDN'T KNOW POSSIBLY HOW BEAUTIFUL SHE IS, COULD YOU? ZELDA WILL BE DOWN IN A MINUTE, AND THEN WATCH ALL THE MEN HERE IN THE LOBBY...

...JUST WATCH THEM WHEN ZELDA GETS OFF THE ELEVATOR.

AND SCOTT ISN'T THE ONLY ONE TO SEE HER BEAUTY.

54

ALL WOMEN ARE BIRDS.

WHAT KIND AM I?

A SWALLOW, I THINK, AND SOMETIMES A BIRD OF PARADISE. MOST GIRLS ARE SPARROWS, OF COURSE...

AND OF COURSE YOU'VE MET CANARY GIRLS—AND ROBIN GIRLS.

AND SWAN GIRLS AND PARROT GIRLS. ALL GROWN WOMEN ARE HAWKS, I THINK, OR OWLS.

SEE THAT ROW OF NURSE-MAIDS OVER THERE? THEY'RE SPARROWS—OR ARE THEY MAGPIES?

AND WHAT AM I—A BUZZARD?

OH, NO, YOU'RE NOT A BIRD AT ALL, DO YOU THINK? YOU'RE A RUSSIAN WOLFHOUND.

ZELDA AND SCOTT LOVE EACH OTHER LIKE MAD. THEY SAY THEIR MARRIAGE WILL LAST.

WHEN THE HONEYMOON IS OVER, THEY BUY A SECOND-HAND MARMON...

...RENT A HOUSE IN CONNECTICUT...

...AND HIRE A JAPANESE BUTLER.

THEY SPEND THE SUMMER WITH FRIENDS, SWIMMING AND READING.

ZELDA IS PICKY ABOUT HER FOOD, WHILE SCOTT ISN'T.

ARE YOU GOING TO EAT THAT?

SCOTT CAN ONLY SLEEP WITH THE WINDOW SHUT, WHILE ZELDA CAN'T SLEEP WITHOUT IT OPEN.

ZELDA CAN'T SEW A BUTTON ON A SHIRT, NOR DOES SHE BOTHER TO SEND OUT THE LAUNDRY. SCOTT LIKES TO CHANGE HIS CLOTHES TWICE A DAY AND CAN'T FIND ANY CLEAN ONES.

ZELDA AND SCOTT FIGHT LIKE MAD. THEY SAY THEIR MARRIAGE CAN'T SUCCEED.

5.

THE HAPPY YEARS

ZELDA MISSES ALABAMA, AND ALABAMA MISSES ZELDA.

IN ALABAMA ALL THE GOOD PEOPLE EAT BISCUITS FOR BREAKFAST, WHICH MAKE THEM VERY BEAUTIFUL AND PLEASANT AND HAPPY, WHILE UP IN CONNECTICUT ALL THE PEOPLE EAT BACON AND EGGS AND TOAST, WHICH MAKE THEM VERY CROSS AND BORED AND MISERABLE.

AND I WISH I COULD HAVE SOME PEACHES ANYHOW.

WE WILL...GET IN OUR CAR... WE WILL DRIVE FROM HERE TO MONTGOMERY, ALABAMA, WHERE WE WILL EAT BISCUITS AND PEACHES.

SO SCOTT AND ZELDA SET OFF...

OH, NO.

...ON "THE CRUISE OF THE ROLLING JUNK."

WE ARE TOURING TO ALABAMA.

WHICH HALF THE CAR YOU GOING IN? THE HIGH HALF OR THE LOW HALF?

YOU BETTER HAVE A HEARSE BODY PUT ON.

58

THEY DRIVE ALL THE WAY TO ALABAMA, BUT RETURN TO CONNECTICUT BY TRAIN. AND SCOTT WILL TURN THAT IMPROBABLE JOURNEY INTO A CHARMING SHORT STORY.

WHEN WE HAVE A BABY, I WANT IT TO LOOK LIKE YOU.

EXCEPT ITS LEGS.

OH, YES, EXCEPT HIS LEGS. BUT THE REST OF HIM CAN BE YOU.

MY NOSE?

WELL, PERHAPS MY NOSE. BUT CERTAINLY YOUR EYES—AND MY MOUTH, AND I GUESS MY SHAPE OF THE FACE. I WONDER; I THINK HE'D BE SORT OF CUTE IF HE HAD MY HAIR.

MY DEAR ZELDA, YOU'VE APPROPRIATED THE WHOLE BABY.

WELL, I DIDN'T MEAN TO.

LET HIM HAVE MY NECK AT LEAST. YOU'VE OFTEN SAID YOU LIKED MY NECK BECAUSE THE ADAM'S APPLE DOESN'T SHOW, AND BESIDES, YOUR NECK'S TOO SHORT.

WHY, IT IS NOT! IT'S JUST RIGHT. I DON'T BELIEVE I'VE EVER SEEN A BETTER NECK.

IT'S TOO SHORT.

SHORT? SHORT? YOU'RE CRAZY! DO YOU CALL THAT A SHORT NECK?

ONE OF THE SHORTEST I'VE EVER SEEN.

OH, SCOTT...

MY LORD, ZELDA! DON'T CRY, PLEASE! DIDN'T YOU KNOW I WAS ONLY KIDDING? ZELDA, LOOK AT ME! WHY, DEAREST, YOU'VE GOT THE LONGEST NECK I'VE EVER SEEN. HONESTLY.

WELL—YOU SHOULDN'T HAVE SAID THAT, THEN.

59

LET'S TALK ABOUT THE B-BABY...

THERE'S THE BABY THAT'S THE COMBINATION OF THE BEST OF BOTH OF US. YOUR BODY, MY EYES, MY MIND, YOUR INTELLIGENCE...

TO PUT IT BRIEFLY, THERE ARE TWO BABIES WE COULD HAVE, TWO DISTINCT AND LOGICAL BABIES, UTTERLY DIFFERENTIATED.

...AND THEN THERE IS THE BABY WHICH IS OUR WORST— MY BODY, YOUR DISPOSITION, AND MY IRRESOLUTION.

I LIKE THAT SECOND BABY.

WHAT I'D REALLY LIKE WOULD BE TO HAVE TWO SETS OF TRIPLETS ONE YEAR APART AND THEN EXPERIMENT WITH THE SIX BOYS—

POOR ME.

—I'D EDUCATE THEM EACH IN A DIFFERENT COUNTRY AND BY A DIFFERENT SYSTEM AND WHEN THEY WERE TWENTY-THREE I'D CALL THEM TOGETHER AND SEE WHAT THEY WERE LIKE.

LET'S HAVE 'EM ALL WITH MY NECK.

ALL I THINK OF EVER IS THAT I LOVE YOU. I VALUE MY BODY BECAUSE YOU THINK IT'S BEAUTIFUL. AND THIS BODY OF MINE—OF YOURS— TO HAVE IT GROW UGLY AND SHAPELESS? IT'S SIMPLY INTOLERABLE. OH, SCOTT, I'M NOT AFRAID OF THE PAIN.

AND THEN AFTERWARD I MIGHT HAVE WIDE HIPS AND BE PALE, WITH ALL MY FRESHNESS GONE AND NO RADIANCE IN MY HAIR.

I DON'T KNOW ANYTHING. I'VE ALWAYS HATED OBSTRICS, OR WHATEVER YOU CALL THEM.

I THOUGHT I'D HAVE A CHILD SOME TIME. BUT NOT NOW.

DO YOU WANT ME TO HAVE IT?

I'M NEUTRAL. IF YOU HAVE IT I'LL PROBABLY BE GLAD. IF YOU DON'T—WELL, THAT'S ALL RIGHT TOO.

I WISH YOU'D MAKE UP YOUR MIND ONE WAY OR THE OTHER!

SUPPOSE YOU MAKE UP YOUR OWN MIND.

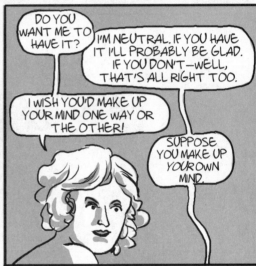

YOU'D THINK YOU'D BEEN SINGLED OUT OF ALL THE WOMEN IN THE WORLD FOR THIS CROWNING INDIGNITY

IT ISN'T AN INDIGNITY FOR THEM. IT'S THEIR ONE EXCUSE FOR LIVING. IT'S THE ONE THING THEY'RE GOOD FOR. IT IS AN INDIGNITY FOR ME.

SEE HERE, ZELDA, I'M WITH YOU WHATEVER YOU DO, BUT FOR GOD'S SAKE BE A SPORT ABOUT IT.

OH, DON'T FUSS AT ME!

YOU SEE, IT ISN'T THAT I'M AFRAID—OF THIS OR ANYTHING ELSE. I'M BEING TRUE TO ME, YOU KNOW.

ON VALENTINE'S DAY, ZELDA FINDS OUT SHE'S PREGNANT.

ON MAY 3, 1921, THE FITZGERALDS BOARD THE *AQUITANIA* AND SAIL TO ENGLAND. THE ACTRESS TALLULAH BANKHEAD, ONE OF ZELDA'S CHILDHOOD FRIENDS, IS ABOARD SHIP WITH THEM.

TALLULAH BANKHEAD

IN LONDON, THEY'RE INVITED TO LUNCH WITH LADY RANDOLPH CHURCHILL AND HER SON WINSTON.

HAVE YOU ALREADY SEEN OXFORD?

OH, YES! SCOTT IS SERIOUSLY THINKING OF GOING TO LIVE THERE.

LOOK, SCOTT!!

LOOK, ZELDA!!

BUT THEY SOON LEAVE ENGLAND AND TRAVEL TO FRANCE, AND THEN, ITALY, VENICE, FLORENCE, ROME...

IN JULY, THEY RETURN TO AMERICA AND MOVE TO MONTGOMERY...

MONTGOMERY

...AND FROM THERE, TO ST. PAUL, MINNESOTA.

ST. PAUL

62

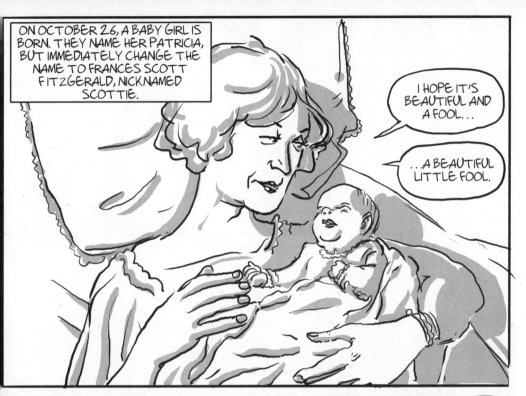

ON OCTOBER 26, A BABY GIRL IS BORN. THEY NAME HER PATRICIA, BUT IMMEDIATELY CHANGE THE NAME TO FRANCES SCOTT FITZGERALD, NICKNAMED SCOTTIE.

I HOPE IT'S BEAUTIFUL AND A FOOL...

...A BEAUTIFUL LITTLE FOOL.

SCOTTIE IS QUICKLY ENTRUSTED TO THE CARE OF A NURSE.

CHILDREN SHOULDN'T BOTHER THEIR PARENTS, NOR PARENTS THEIR CHILDREN.

ZELDA CAN'T STAND BEING OVERWEIGHT, AND IN HER PICTURES, SHE RETOUCHES HER NOSE, CHEEKS, AND CHIN.

THERE, THAT'S BETTER.

63

IN MARCH 1922, THE *BEATIFUL AND DAMNED* IS PUBLISHED.

THE BEAUTIFUL AND DAMNED
BY THE AUTHOR OF "THIS SIDE OF PARADISE"

For my darling wife, my dearest sweetest baboo, without whose love and aid neither this book nor any other would ever have been possible. From me, who loves her more every day, with a heartful of worship for her lovely self.

Scott

St. Paul, Minn.
Feb 6th 1922

THE BEAUTIFUL AND DAMNED
F. Scott Fitzgerald

TO BEGIN WITH, EVERY ONE MUST BUY THIS BOOK FOR THE FOLLOWING AESTHETIC REASONS: FIRST, BECAUSE I KNOW WHERE THERE IS THE CUTEST CLOTH OF GOLD DRESS FOR ONLY $300... AND ALSO IF ENOUGH PEOPLE BUY IT, WHERE THERE IS A PLATINUM RING WITH A COMPLETE CIRCLET, AND ALSO IF LOADS OF PEOPLE BUY IT MY HUSBAND NEEDS A NEW WINTER OVERCOAT, ALTHOUGH THE ONE HE HAS HAS DONE WELL ENOUGH FOR THE LAST THREE YEARS.

IT SEEMS TO ME THAT ON ONE PAGE I RECOGNIZED A PORTION OF AN OLD DIARY OF MINE WHICH MYSTERIOUSLY DISAPPEARED SHORTLY AFTER MY MARRIAGE, AND ALSO SCRAPS OF LETTERS WHICH, THOUGH CONSIDERABLY EDITED, SOUND TO ME VAGUELY FAMILIAR.

IN FACT, MR. FITZGERALD—I BELIEVE THAT IS HOW HE SPELLS HIS NAME—SEEMS TO BELIEVE THAT PLAGIARISM BEGINS AT HOME.

THE *NEW YORK TRIBUNE* ASKS ZELDA TO REVIEW HER HUSBAND'S BOOK...

64

SEE IF THERE IS ANY BACON...

THEN ASK IF THERE ARE ANY EGGS, AND IF SO TRY AND PERSUADE THE COOK TO POACH TWO OF THEM.

...AND IF THERE IS ASK THE COOK WHICH PAN TO FRY IT IN.

COOK

IT IS BETTER NOT TO ATTEMPT TOAST, AS IT BURNS VERY EASILY.

ALSO, IN THE CASE OF BACON DO NOT TURN THE FIRE TOO HIGH...

...OR YOU WILL HAVE TO GET OUT OF THE HOUSE FOR A WEEK.

SERVE PREFERABLY ON CHINA PLATES...

...AND HARPER & BROTHERS ASKS HER FOR A RECIPE TO INCLUDE IN *FAVORITE RECIPES OF FAMOUS WOMEN.*

...THOUGH GOLD OR WOOD WILL DO—IF HANDY.

65

WOULD YOU LIKE A ZELDA CUT, TOO?

WOMEN LOVE ZELDA...

I LOATHE WOMEN.

WHAT ON EARTH CAN YOU SAY TO THEM—EXCEPT TALK "LADY-LADY"?

I'VE ENTHUSED OVER A DOZEN BABIES THAT I'VE WANTED ONLY TO CHOKE. AND EVERY ONE OF THOSE GIRLS IS EITHER INCIPIENTLY JEALOUS AND SUSPICIOUS OF HER HUSBAND IF HE'S CHARMING OR BEGINNING TO BE BORED WITH HIM IF HE ISN'T.

DON'T YOU EVER INTEND TO SEE ANY WOMEN?

I DON'T KNOW.

...BUT ZELDA HATES WOMEN.

66

6.

BEFORE THE CRACK-UP

IN JUNE 1922, ZELDA PUBLISHES "EULOGY ON THE FLAPPER" IN *METROPOLITAN MAGAZINE*.

FLAPPERDOM...IS MAKING YOUNG WOMEN INTELLIGENT AND TEACHING THEM TO CAPITALIZE THEIR NATURAL RESOURCES.

THE FLAPPER AWOKE FROM HER LETHARGY OF SUB-DEB-ISM, BOBBED HER HAIR, PUT ON HER CHOICEST PAIR OF EARRINGS AND A GREAT DEAL OF AUDACITY AND ROUGE, AND WENT INTO THE BATTLE.

SHE FLIRTED BECAUSE IT WAS FUN TO FLIRT AND WORE A ONE-PIECE BATHING SUIT BECAUSE SHE HAD A GOOD FIGURE, SHE COVERED HER FACE WITH POWDER AND PAINT BECAUSE SHE DIDN'T NEED IT AND SHE REFUSED TO BE BORED CHIEFLY BECAUSE SHE WASN'T BORING.

SHE WAS CONSCIOUS THAT THE THINGS SHE DID WERE THE THINGS SHE HAD ALWAYS WANTED TO DO.

MOTHERS DISAPPROVED OF THEIR SONS TAKING THE FLAPPER TO DANCES, TO TEAS, TO SWIM AND MOST OF ALL TO HEART.

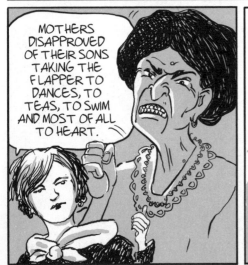

SHE HAD MOSTLY MASCULINE FRIENDS, BUT YOUTH DOES NOT NEED FRIENDS— IT NEEDS ONLY CROWDS.

EVERYTHING ZELDA FITZGERALD SAYS AND DOES STANDS OUT.

THAT SUMMER, SCOTT AND ZELDA MOVE TO THE YACHT CLUB ON WHITE BEAR LAKE, ALSO IN MINNESOTA.

THEY CREATE SUCH A FRIGHTFUL RUCKUS AT ALL HOURS...

...THEY'RE ASKED TO LEAVE.

THEY MOVE NEARBY.

IT SAYS IN THE PAPER WE'RE FAMOUS.

HOW NICE... LET'S SEE...

NICE! BUT IT SAYS WE'RE IN A SANATORIUM FOR WICKEDNESS. WHAT'LL OUR PARENTS THINK WHEN THEY SEE THAT, I'D LIKE TO KNOW!

WELL, THEY'VE THOUGHT WE OUGHT TO BE THERE FOR MONTHS.

69

IN SEPTEMBER, THEY'RE BACK IN NEW YORK, AND THE CITY IS ALL ABUZZ ABOUT ZELDA AGAIN.

I MET THEM TOGETHER FOR THE FIRST TIME AT THE PLAZA... SCOTT CALLED AND ASKED ME IF I WOULD CARE TO JOIN HIM FOR LUNCH... AND I DID... SHE WAS VERY BEAUTIFUL, SHE POSSESSED A SORT OF GRACE... GOOD LOOKING HAIR—EVERYTHING ABOUT HER WAS VERY ORIGINAL AND AMUSING. BUT THERE WAS ALSO THIS LITTLE STRANGE STREAK.

JOHN DOS PASSOS

I HAD BEEN TOLD THAT SHE WAS VERY BEAUTIFUL, BUT WHEN I WENT TO A PARTY AND SAW HER I HAD QUITE A SHOCK. SHE WAS STANDING WITH HER BACK TO ME, AND HER HAIR WAS QUITE LOVELY... I AM SURE THIS WAS NATURAL. THEN SHE TURNED ROUND AND HER FACE HAD A CERTAIN CRAGGY HOMELINESS...

I DON'T GIVE A DAMN.

...SUCH AS ONE SEES IN GERICAULT'S PICTURES OF THE INSANE. HER PROFILE SEEMED ON TWO DIFFERENT PLANES... BUT SHE WAS NOT AT ALL UNLIKABLE. THERE WAS SOMETHING VERY APPEALING ABOUT HER. BUT FRIGHTENING.

REBECCA WEST

SHE WAS AN ORIGINAL. SCOTT WAS NOT A WISE-CRACKER LIKE ZELDA. WHY, SHE TORE UP THE PAVEMENTS WITH SLY REMARKS. SHE TAUNTED BELLBOYS AND WAITERS—JUST, MAYBE, TO SEE WHAT WOULD HAPPEN. SHE DIDN'T ACTUALLY WRITE THEM DOWN, SCOTT DID, BUT SHE SAID THEM.

CARL VAN VECHTEN

IN OCTOBER, THEY RENT A HOUSE ON LONG ISLAND FOR $300 A MONTH...

...AND FIND A NURSE FOR $90 A MONTH...

...A HOUSEKEEPING COUPLE FOR $160 A MONTH...

...AND A WASHERWOMAN FOR $36 A MONTH.

THEY ALSO BUY A SECONDHAND ROLLS-ROYCE.

71

IT BECOMES A HABIT FOR MANY WORLD-WEARY NEW YORKERS TO SPEND WEEKENDS AT THE FITZGERALDS' COUNTRY HOUSE.

SCOTT REFERS TO THEIR LIFE AS THAT OF THE "NEWLY RICH."

THAT IS TO SAY, FIVE YEARS AGO WE HAD NO MONEY AT ALL, AND WHAT WE NOW DO AWAY WITH WOULD HAVE SEEMED LIKE INESTIMABLE RICHES TO US THEN.

I HAVE AT TIMES SUSPECTED THAT WE ARE THE ONLY NEWLY RICH PEOPLE IN AMERICA, THAT IN FACT WE ARE THE VERY COUPLE AT WHOM ALL THE ARTICLES ABOUT THE NEWLY RICH WERE AIMED.

MONEY? WHEN WE HAVE IT, WE SPEND IT.

IN THE FALL OF 1923, THE *BALTIMORE SUN* SENDS A CORRESPONDENT TO INTERVIEW ZELDA.

I LIKE TO WRITE.

DO YOU KNOW, I THOUGHT MY HUSBAND SHOULD WRITE A PERFECTLY GOOD ENDING TO ONE OF THE TALES, AND HE WOULDN'T! HE CALLED THEM "LOP-SIDED," TOO! SAID THAT THEY BEGAN AT THE END.

I LOVE SCOTT'S BOOKS AND HEROINES.

I LIKE THE ONES THAT ARE LIKE ME! THAT'S WHY I LOVE ROSALIND IN *THIS SIDE OF PARADISE*.

I LIKE GIRLS LIKE THAT. I LIKE THEIR COURAGE, THEIR RECKLESSNESS AND SPENDTHRIFTNESS. ROSALIND WAS THE ORIGINAL AMERICAN FLAPPER.

ZELDA ASKS SCOTT TO GIVE HER A HAND IN TRANSFORMING THE INTERVIEW INTO A DIALOGUE BETWEEN HUSBAND AND WIFE.

I REFUSE TO AMPLIFY. EXCEPTING— SHE'S PERFECT.

BUT YOU DON'T THINK THAT. YOU THINK I'M A LAZY WOMAN.

NO, I LIKE IT... YOU'RE ALWAYS READY TO LISTEN TO MY MANUSCRIPTS AT ANY HOUR OF THE DAY OR NIGHT. YOU'RE CHARMING—BEAUTIFUL YOU DO, I BELIEVE, CLEAN THE ICE BOX ONCE A WEEK.

WHOM DO YOU CONSIDER THE MOST INTERESTING CHARACTER IN FICTION?

BECKY SHARP IN *VANITY FAIR*. ONLY, I DO WISH SHE'D BEEN PRETTY.

73

WHAT WOULD YOUR IDEAL DAY CONSTITUTE?

PEACHES FOR BREAKFAST... THEN GOLF. THEN A SWIM. THEN JUST BEING LAZY. NOT EATING OR READING, BUT BEING QUIET AND HEARING PLEASANT SOUNDS—RATHER A TOTAL VACUITY. THE EVENING? A LARGE, BRILLIANT GATHERING, I BELIEVE.

ARE YOU AMBITIOUS?

NOT ESPECIALLY, BUT I'VE PLENTY OF HOPE. I DON'T WANT TO BELONG TO CLUBS. NO COMMITTEES. I'M NOT A JOINER. JUST BE MYSELF AND ENJOY LIVING.

WHAT DO YOU WANT YOUR DAUGHTER TO DO, MRS. FITZGERALD, WHEN SHE GROWS UP?

NOT GREAT AND SERIOUS AND MELANCHOLY AND INHOSPITABLE, BUT RICH AND HAPPY AND ARTISTIC. I DON'T MEAN THAT MONEY MEANS HAPPINESS, NECESSARILY. BUT HAVING THINGS, JUST THINGS, OBJECTS MAKE A WOMAN HAPPY. THE RIGHT KIND OF PERFUME, THE SMART PAIR OF SHOES. THEY ARE GREAT COMFORTS TO THE FEMININE SOUL... I'D RATHER HAVE HER BE A MARILYN MILLER THAN A PAVLOVA.

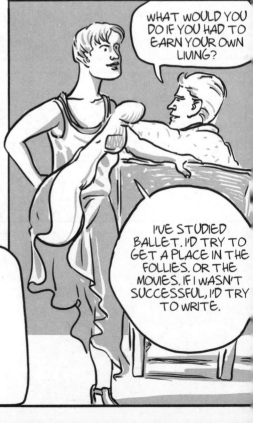

WHAT WOULD YOU DO IF YOU HAD TO EARN YOUR OWN LIVING?

I'VE STUDIED BALLET. I'D TRY TO GET A PLACE IN THE FOLLIES. OR THE MOVIES. IF I WASN'T SUCCESSFUL, I'D TRY TO WRITE.

74

BUT THEY'RE BOTH ALREADY WRITING...

BETWEEN 1922 AND 1923, I EARN $1,300 FROM TWO SHORT STORIES, A REVIEW, AND A COUPLE OF ARTICLES.

...DRINKING...

HOW TO MAKE A GIN RICKEY...

PUT SOME ICE IN A GLASS WITH THE JUICE OF HALF A LEMON. ADD GIN, SODA WATER, AND A SLICE OF LIME.

...AND THEY LOVE PARTIES.

OH, GOOFO, I'M DRUNK...

BUT FAME DOESN'T MAKE THEM HAPPY...

OUR ROLE WILL ALWAYS BE DISCOUNTING THE CHARACTER THEY THINK WE ARE FROM NOW ON.

HASN'T IT ALWAYS BEEN?

75

...AND NEITHER DO PARTIES.

YOU WANT PARTIES AS MUCH AS I DO.

EVERYTHING I DO IS IN ACCORDANCE WITH MY IDEAS: TO USE EVERY MINUTE OF THESE YEARS, WHEN I'M YOUNG, IN HAVING THE BEST TIME I POSSIBLY CAN.

HOW ABOUT AFTER THAT?

AFTER THAT I WON'T CARE.

THEY FIGHT...

UTTERLY OUTRAGEOUS!

MOST CERTAINLY.

IT'S SO, NEVERTHE-LESS...

REGARDLESS.

...AND THEY MAKE UP.

DARLING, I WISH I COULD LIVE IN YOUR POCKET.

DARLING, THERE'D BE A HOLE YOU'D FORGOTTEN TO DARN AND YOU'D SLIP THROUGH AND BE BROUGHT HOME BY THE VILLAGE BARBER.

7.

VIVE LA FRANCE!

IN APRIL 1924, FRUSTRATED BY THE IMPOSSIBILITY OF SURVIVING ECONOMICALLY IN AMERICA, SCOTT AND ZELDA MOVE TO FRANCE, WHERE THE RATE OF EXCHANGE IS NINETEEN FRANCS TO THE DOLLAR.

SUMMER AND LOVE AND BEAUTY ARE MUCH THE SAME IN CANNES OR CONNECTICUT.

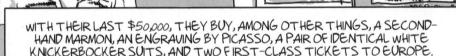

WITH THEIR LAST $50,000, THEY BUY, AMONG OTHER THINGS, A SECOND-HAND MARMON, AN ENGRAVING BY PICASSO, A PAIR OF IDENTICAL WHITE KNICKERBOCKER SUITS, AND TWO FIRST-CLASS TICKETS TO EUROPE.

EVERYONE SAYS THEY WISH THEY COULD COME WITH THEM.

BYE-BYE.

78

ZELDA, SCOTT, AND SCOTTIE DISEMBARK IN PARIS.

I THINK FOUR MEN HAVE DISCOVERED PARIS TO ONE THAT DISCOVERED GOD.

THEY REDISCOVER OLD FRIENDS.

THIS, LAWTON, IS MY JEANNE D'ARC DRESS.

LAWTON CAMPBELL

THEY WERE SO SMARTLY DRESSED AND STRIKING... THEY WERE BEAUTIFUL—THE LOVELINESS... SHE WAS DRESSED IN A LOVELY FROCK WHICH SHE HAD DESIGNED.

AND THEY MAKE NEW ONES.

BISTROT LES SANS CULOTTES

LIVING WELL IS THE BEST REVENGE.

HOTEL

PARIS WAS LIKE A GREAT FAIR, AND EVERYBODY WAS SO YOUNG.

I DON'T THINK WE COULD HAVE TAKEN SCOTT ALONE. ZELDA HAD HER OWN PERSONAL STYLE... SHE MIGHT DRESS LIKE A FLAPPER WHEN IT WAS APPROPRIATE TO DO SO, BUT ALWAYS WITH A DIFFERENCE. ACTUALLY, HER TASTE WAS NEVER WHAT ONE WOULD SPEAK OF AS A LA MODE— IT WAS BETTER, IT WAS HER OWN.

GERALD & SARA MURPHY

HERE, THEY MEET PABLO PICASSO...

...COLE PORTER...

...ARCHIBALD MACLEISH...

...FERNAND LÉGER...

...ROBERT BENCHLEY...

...RUDOLPH VALENTINO...

...AND KIKI DE MONTPARNASSE.

A YOUNG AND ATTRACTIVE STREETWALKER WHO POSED FOR ANY PAINTER WHO CAME ALONG— SO INTOXICATED THAT HER FATE WAS ALREADY OBVIOUS.

80

IN MAY, THEY LEAVE FOR THE SOUTH OF FRANCE.

WE TRAVEL PAST THE DELICATE TRACERY OF PARIS...

...AND THE HIGH TERRACES OF LYON...

...THE BELFRIES OF DIJON...

...AND THE WHITE ROMANCE OF AVIGNON...

...INTO THE SCENT OF LEMON, THE RUSTLE OF BLACK FOLIAGE...

...CLOUDS OF MOTHS WHIPPING THE HELIOTROPE DUSK INTO PROVENCE.

81

THEY MOVE TO SAINT-RAPHAEL AND RENT THE VILLA MARIE.

I LIKE IT.

SCOTT WRITES *THE GREAT GATSBY.*

ZELDA SWIMS...

...AND GETS BORED.

BECAUSE THE SUN WAS GOOD FOR THEM.

A SMALL HORDE OF PEOPLE WASTED THEIR TIME BEING HAPPY AND WASTED THEIR HAPPINESS BEING TIME BESIDE THE BAKED PALMS AND VINES BRITTLELY CLAWING THE CLAY BANKS.

82

PERHAPS IT IS BOREDOM THAT DRIVES ZELDA TO FALL IN LOVE WITH A FRENCH AVIATOR IN JULY.

OH!

A SHINING BEAUTY.

EDOUARD JOZAN

83

JOZAN WASN'T SOMEONE FOR HER TO TALK TO...

SARA MURPHY

...I MUST SAY EVERYONE KNEW ABOUT IT BUT SCOTT.

GERALD MURPHY

I DON'T KNOW HOW FAR IT REALLY WENT, I SUSPECT IT WASN'T MUCH, BUT IT DID UPSET SCOTT A GOOD DEAL. I WONDER WHETHER IT WASN'T PARTLY HIS OWN FAULT?

EDOUARD JOZAN

ONE DAY THE FITZGERALDS LEFT AND THEIR FRIENDS SCATTERED, EACH TO HIS OWN DESTINY.

84

IN SEPTEMBER, ZELDA ATTEMPTS SUICIDE.

I KNEW SOMETHING HAD HAPPENED THAT COULD NEVER BE REPAIRED.

85

IN OCTOBER, ALMOST EVERYTHING IS BACK TO NORMAL.

YOU'RE A ROTTEN DRIVER. EITHER YOU OUGHT TO BE MORE CAREFUL, OR YOU OUGHTN'T TO DRIVE AT ALL.

I AM CAREFUL!

NO, YOU'RE NOT.

WELL, OTHER PEOPLE ARE.

WHAT'S THAT GOT TO DO WITH IT?

THEY'LL KEEP OUT OF MY WAY. IT TAKES TWO TO MAKE AN ACCIDENT.

SUPPOSE YOU MET SOMEBODY JUST AS CARELESS AS YOURSELF.

I HOPE I NEVER WILL.

I HATE CARELESS PEOPLE. THAT'S WHY I LIKE YOU.

86

8.

ITALIAN JOURNEY

AT THE BEGINNING OF NOVEMBER 1924, THEY MOVE TO ITALY, WHERE THE EXCHANGE RATE IS EVEN BETTER THAN IN FRANCE.

ROMA

I LIKE FRANCE, WHERE EVERYBODY THINKS HE'S NAPOLEON—DOWN HERE EVERYBODY THINKS HE'S CHRIST.

THEY STAY AT THE HOTEL DES PRINCES, AT THE FOOT OF THE SPANISH STEPS. AT NIGHT, THE SHEETS ARE DAMP, AND THEY CAN HEAR OTHER PEOPLE SNORING.

BY DAY, THEY EAT BEL PAESE CHEESE AND DRINK CORVO WINE.

88

NEITHER OF THEM LOVE ROME.

THE CHURCH IS A LITTLE LIKE THE THEATER, ISN'T IT? IT SHOULD BE A LITTLE MORE SELECTIVE IN CASTING ITS ACTORS.

SCOTT DRINKS...

...ZELDA GETS SICK.

AND WHEN THEY RUN THROUGH THEIR SAVINGS, SCOTT IS FORCED TO WRITE SHORT STORIES...

...WHILE ZELDA, ALL BETTER NOW, TOURS THE CITY.

IT WAS EXCITING BEING LOST BETWEEN CENTURIES IN THE ROMAN DUSK AND TAKING YOUR SENSE OF DIRECTION FROM THE COLOSSEUM.

89

TOGETHER THEY COME UP WITH TITLES FOR SCOTT'S NEW NOVEL.

I COULD CALL IT TRIMALCHIO IN WEST EGG.

OR, PERHAPS, TRIMALCHIO.

OR GATSBY.

OR GOLD-HATTED GATSBY.

OR THE HIGH-BOUNCING LOVER.

I LIKE THE GREAT GATSBY.

AT CHRISTMAS, THEY ATTEND A PARTY AT THE EXCELSIOR FOR THE FILM *BEN HUR*.

SCOTT FLIRTS WITH THE ACTRESS CARMEL MYERS.

DO YOU KNOW WHAT THESE OLD ROMAN FAMILIES ARE? THEY'RE BANDITS, THEY'RE THE ONES WHO GOT POSSESSION OF THE TEMPLES AND PALACES AFTER ROME WENT TO PIECES AND PREYED ON THE PEOPLE.

AND ZELDA RETALIATES BY ASKING THE JOURNALIST HOWARD COXE TO SEE HER BACK TO THE HOTEL.

BYE-BYE, SCOTT.

IN JANUARY, BORED, THEY GO ON EXCURSIONS TO FRASCATI...

...TIVOLI.

...AND NAPLES.

92

WHEN THEY RETURN TO ROME, SCOTT GETS IN A FISTFIGHT WITH A TAXI-DRIVER, WHO TRIES TO CHEAT HIM...

CRIMINAL!

...AND IS BEATEN UP AND ARRESTED.

ROMA

IT'S THEIR FAREWELL TO ROME.

93

IN FEBRUARY, THEY'RE IN CAPRI, AT THE HOTEL TIBERIO PALACE...

HOW LOVELY THIS IS, SCOTT!

...WHERE THEY SPEND THEIR TIME FIGHTING.

ZELDA AND I SOMETIMES INDULGE IN TERRIBLE FOUR-DAY ROWS THAT ALWAYS START WITH A DRINKING PARTY, BUT WE'RE STILL ENORMOUSLY IN LOVE AND ABOUT THE ONLY TRULY HAPPILY MARRIED PEOPLE I KNOW.

94

SCOTT AND ZELDA MEET COMPTON MACKENZIE. HE INTRODUCES THEM TO A COMMUNITY OF HOMOSEXUAL ENGLISH INTELLECTUALS, WHO'VE MOVED TO THE TOLERANT ISLE OF CAPRI. HERE, THEY ENJOY THEMSELVES WITH AN ARRAY OF GOSSIP, PARTIES, WINE, OPIUM, AND COCAINE.

FAY MACKENZIE

COMPTON MACKENZIE

NATALIE BARNEY

SCOTT

ROMAINE BROOKS

WILLIAM SOMERSET MAUGHAM

NORMAN DOUGLAS

JOHN ELLINGHAM BROOKS

ZELDA

E.F.BENSON

ZELDA TAKES HER FIRST PAINTING LESSONS.

SHE PAINTS FLOWERS, MOSTLY NASTURTIUMS.

95

IN APRIL 1925, THE GREAT GATSBY IS PUBLISHED.

IT SEEMS TO ME TO BE THE FIRST STEP THAT AMERICAN FICTION HAS TAKEN SINCE HENRY JAMES.

T.S. ELIOT

The GREAT GATSBY

F. Scott Fitzgerald

IN APRIL, THEY DECIDE TO GO BACK TO FRANCE. THEY BOARD A BOAT FOR MARSEILLES IN NAPLES.

DURING THE DRIVE NORTH, THE CAR'S CANVAS ROOF IS DAMAGED, AND THEY'RE FORCED TO DRIVE WITH THE TOP DOWN.

WHEN THEY REACH LYONS, THEY ABANDON THE CAR...

...AND CONTINUE ON TO PARIS BY TRAIN, FOR A SPRING OF...

...1,000 PARTIES AND NO WORK.

96

9.

BACK IN FRANCE

BACK IN PARIS, THE FITZGERALDS LET AN APARTMENT AT 14, RUE DE TILSITT, NEAR THE PLACE DE L'ÉTOILE.

SCOTT MEETS SYLVIA BEACH AND STARTS SPENDING TIME AT HER BOOKSTORE, SHAKESPEARE AND COMPANY.

DINGO AMERICAN BAR AND RESTAURANT

AT THE DINGO BAR, HE MAKES FRIENDS WITH ERNEST HEMINGWAY, WHO IS THREE YEARS YOUNGER THAN HIM AND A GOOD SIX INCHES TALLER.

IF YOU ARE LUCKY ENOUGH TO HAVE LIVED IN PARIS AS A YOUNG MAN, THEN WHEREVER YOU GO FOR THE REST OF YOUR LIFE IT STAYS WITH YOU, FOR PARIS IS A MOVEABLE FEAST.

SCOTT WAS A MAN THEN WHO LOOKED LIKE A BOY WITH A FACE BETWEEN HANDSOME AND PRETTY.

AT THAT TIME SCOTT HATED THE FRENCH, AND SINCE ALMOST THE ONLY FRENCH HE MET WITH REGULARLY WERE WAITERS WHOM HE DID NOT UNDERSTAND, TAXI-DRIVERS, GARAGE EMPLOYEES AND LANDLORDS, HE HAD MANY OPPORTUNITIES TO INSULT AND ABUSE THEM.

HE TOLD ME THAT HE AND ZELDA...HAD BEEN COMPELLED TO ABANDON THEIR SMALL RENAULT MOTOR CAR IN LYON BECAUSE OF BAD WEATHER AND HE ASKED ME IF I WOULD GO DOWN TO LYON WITH HIM ON THE TRAIN TO PICK UP THE CAR AND DRIVE UP WITH HIM TO PARIS.

BECOMING UNCONSCIOUS WHEN THEY DRANK HAD ALWAYS BEEN THEIR GREAT DEFENSE. THEY WENT TO SLEEP ON DRINKING AN AMOUNT OF LIQUOR OR CHAMPAGNE THAT WOULD HAVE LITTLE EFFECT ON A PERSON ACCUSTOMED TO DRINKING, AND THEY WOULD GO TO SLEEP LIKE CHILDREN.

99

ZELDA MEETS HADLEY RICHARDSON, HEMINGWAY'S FIRST WIFE.

I NOTICE THAT IN THE HEMINGWAY FAMILY YOU DO WHAT ERNEST WANTS.

A CHARMING, LOVELY CREATURE. SHE LIVED ON WHAT ERNEST CALLED THE "FESTIVAL CONCEPTION OF LIFE"...A FRIVOLOUS KIND OF WOMAN. THEY WERE INCONVENIENT FRIENDS.

THEY WOULD CALL ON THE HEMINGWAYS AT FOUR 'OCLOCK IN THE MORNING AND WE HAD A BABY AND DIDN'T APPRECIATE IT VERY MUCH. WHEN SCOTT WROTE I DON'T KNOW.

HADLEY RICHARDSON

IN MAY, HEMINGWAY INTRODUCES SCOTT AND ZELDA TO GERTRUDE STEIN AND ALICE TOKLAS.

HERE WE ARE AND HAVE READ YOUR BOOK AND IT IS A GOOD BOOK...

...YOU ARE CREATING THE CONTEMPORARY WORLD MUCH AS THACKERAY DID HIS IN PENDENNIS AND VANITY FAIR AND THIS ISN'T A BAD COMPLIMENT.

100

ZELDA IS JEALOUS OF SCOTT'S WORK, WHILE SCOTT IS JEALOUS OF ZELDA. ZELDA TRIES TO KEEP SCOTT FROM WRITING, AND SCOTT TRIES TO KEEP ZELDA FROM SEEING OTHER PEOPLE.

AFTER THE SPRING, IT IS THE SUMMER OF 1,000 PARTIES AND NO WORK.

EVEN AS A MOTHER, ZELDA CONTINUES TO BE OSTENTATIOUSLY FLAPPERISH.

I'M RAISING MY GIRL TO BE A FLAPPER. I LIKE THE JAZZ GENERATION, AND I HOPE MY DAUGHTER'S GENERATION WILL BE JAZZIER. I WANT MY GIRL TO DO AS SHE PLEASES, BE WHAT SHE PLEASES, REGARDLESS OF MRS. GRUNDY.

I THINK A WOMAN GETS MORE HAPPINESS OUT OF BEING GAY, LIGHT-HEARTED, UNCONVENTIONAL, MISTRESS OF HER OWN FATE, THAN OUT OF A CAREER THAT CALLS FOR HARD WORK, INTELLECTUAL PESSIMISM AND LONELINESS. I DON'T WANT SCOTTIE TO BE A GENIUS. I WANT HER TO BE A FLAPPER, BECAUSE FLAPPERS ARE BRAVE AND GAY AND BEAUTIFUL.

101

IN AUGUST, THEY LEAVE FOR CAP D'ANTIBES.

ONE COULD GET AWAY WITH MORE ON THE SUMMER RIVIERA, AND WHATEVER HAPPENED SEEMED TO HAVE SOMETHING TO DO WITH ART.

AND IN SEPTEMBER, THEY RETURN TO THE APARTMENT ON THE RUE DE TILSITT IN PARIS.

A FIVE-FLIGHT WALK-UP WITH FADED GOLD-AND-PURPLE WALLPAPER.

ZELDA STARTS TAKING DANCE LESSONS.

ALLONGÉE.

TAP

IN MARCH, THEY'RE BACK ON THE COTE D'AZUR, IN JUAN-LES-PINS, WITH THE MURPHYS.

HER BEAUTY...WAS ALL IN HER EYES. THEY WERE STRANGE EYES, BROODING BUT NOT SAD, SEVERE, ALMOST MASCULINE IN THEIR DIRECTNESS... IF SHE LOOKED LIKE ANYTHING IT WAS AN AMERICAN INDIAN.

SHE SEEMED SOMETIMES TO BE LYING IN AMBUSH WAITING FOR YOU.

SHE WAS THE ONLY WOMAN I'VE EVER KNOWN WHO COULD WEAR A PEONY IN HER HAIR OR ON HER SHOULDER AND NOT LOOK SILLY.

THEY WOULD BEGIN TOGETHER IN THE EVENING; YOU WOULD SEE SOME LOOK COME OVER THEM AS THOUGH THEY HAD BEEN DRAWN TOGETHER— AND THEN THEY WERE COMPANIONS. THEN THEY WERE INSEPARABLE.

WE KNEW THEY ROWED, ALL MARRIED PEOPLE ROW, DON'T THEY? OH, THEY DID HAVE TERRIFIC ROWS, BUT NEVER IN PUBLIC AND NEVER IN FRONT OF THEIR FRIENDS. ONE HEARD OF IT THE NEXT DAY; OR ONE SAW ZELDA'S TRUNK OUT ON THE STREET WHERE SHE HAD LEFT IT THE NIGHT BEFORE.

THERE SHE WOULD WAIT— ONE NEVER KNEW WHAT FOR. WHEN SHE GOT SLEEPY SHE'D GO BACK TO BED, BUT THE TRUNK WAS LEFT BEHIND. ONE ALWAYS KNEW WHEN THE FITZGERALDS HAD ROWED; THE TRUNK MARKED THE NIGHT.

103

IN MAY, THE HEMINGWAYS JOIN THEM ON THE COTE D'AZUR. AND THERE THEY STAY UNTIL THE END OF 1926.

ZELDA IS JEALOUS OF HEMINGWAY. HEMINGWAY DETESTS ZELDA.

ZELDA WAS VERY BEAUTIFUL AND WAS TANNED A LOVELY GOLD COLOR AND HER HAIR WAS A BEAUTIFUL DARK GOLD AND SHE WAS VERY FRIENDLY. HER HAWK'S EYES WERE CLEAR AND CALM.

I KNEW EVERYTHING WAS ALL RIGHT AND WAS GOING TO TURN OUT WELL IN THE END WHEN SHE LEANED FORWARD AND SAID TO ME, TELLING ME HER GREAT SECRET, "ERNEST, DON'T YOU THINK THAT AL JOLSON IS GREATER THAN JESUS?"

IT WAS ONLY ZELDA'S SECRET THAT SHE SHARED WITH ME, AS A HAWK MIGHT SHARE SOMETHING WITH A MAN. BUT HAWKS DO NOT SHARE SCOTT DID NOT WRITE ANYTHING ANY MORE THAT WAS GOOD UNTIL AFTER HE KNEW THAT SHE WAS INSANE.

19

ONE NIGHT THAT SUMMER, WHILE HAVING DINNER IN SAINT-PAUL DE VENCE, IN THE MOUNTAINS ABOVE NICE, THEY SEE ISADORA DUNCAN AT A NEARBY TABLE.

LOOK, IT'S ISADORA DUNCAN...

SCOTT, STARSTRUCK, GOES OVER TO EXPRESS HIS ADMIRATION.

OH, YOU'RE MY CENTURION!

IN A JEALOUS FIT, ZELDA JUMPS OVER THE WALL AND DOWN A STAIRWELL.

OH, NO!!

ZELDA!!

THEY DIDN'T WANT ORDINARY PLEASURES, THEY HARDLY NOTICED GOOD FOOD OR WINES, BUT THEY DID WANT SOMETHING TO HAPPEN.

THEY ARE RENOWN ON THE COTE D'AZUR FOR THEIR DARING HIGH DIVES INTO THE SEA. ZELDA ALWAYS CHALLENGES SCOTT, AND SCOTT ALWAYS FOLLOWS HER.

I REMEMBER ONE EVENING WHEN I WAS WITH THEM THAT HE WAS ABSOLUTELY TREMBLING WHEN SHE CHALLENGED HIM, BUT HE FOLLOWED HER. IT WAS BREATHTAKING. THEY TOOK EACH DIVE, RETURNING FROM THE SEA ALL SHIVERING AND WHITE.

SARA MURPHY

I DIDN'T THINK HE COULD GO THROUGH WITH IT, BUT HE DID. AND THAT WAS THAT.

WE ASKED A LOT OF LIFE AND GAVE FREELY OF WHAT WE HAD... SO WE LIVED CUTTING OFF THE COMPLICATED AND REPLACING IT WITH THE SIMPLE TILL THERE WAS LITTLE LEFT.

GOD, HOW MUCH I'VE LEARNED IN THESE TWO AND A HALF YEARS IN EUROPE. IT SEEMS LIKE A DECADE AND I FEEL PRETTY OLD BUT I WOULDN'T HAVE MISSED IT, EVEN ITS MOST UNPLEASANT AND PAINFUL ASPECTS.

106

10.

HOLLYWOOD

I ALWAYS THOUGHT THAT THOSE LONG CONVERSATIONS THAT STARTED AT MIDNIGHT...

...AND WENT ON UNTIL THE FIRST LIGHT OF DAWN SENT US SCURRYING TO SLEEP...

...WERE AN ESSENTIAL PART OF OUR RELATIONSHIP...

...A KIND OF INTIMACY THAT WE NEVER FOUND IN OUR EVERYDAY MARRIED LIFE.

BUT THOSE CONVERSATIONS BROKE OFF SOMEWHERE IN EUROPE.

IN DECEMBER 1926, ZELDA AND SCOTT RETURN TO THE UNITED STATES.

108

SCOTT AND ZELDA GO TO LOS ANGELES AND LIVE IN A BUNGALOW AT THE AMBASSADOR HOTEL, WITH POLA NEGRI AND JOHN BARRYMORE FOR NEIGHBORS.

WE WENT BACK TO AMERICA, FURTHER APART THAN WE HAD EVER BEEN BEFORE.

THE PEOPLE OF HOLLYWOOD ARE NOT VERY NICE OUTWARDLY—THERE IS TOO MUCH UNWELCOME FAMILIARITY, TOO MUCH CASUAL SNOOTINESS.

THEY SUDDENLY REALIZE THEY NO LONGER HAVE ANYTHING TO SAY TO EACH OTHER.

SCOTT GETS A JOB AS A SCREENWRITER FOR UNITED ARTISTS, WORKING ON AN ORIGINAL SCREENPLAY ABOUT FLAPPERS.

BUT THE SCRIPT, TITLED LIPSTICK, NEVER BECOMES A MOVIE.

WHILE SCOTT WRITES FOR THE MOVIES, ZELDA WRITES TO SCOTTIE, WHO'S BACK IN WASHINGTON WITH HER GRANDPARENTS.

LAST NIGHT WE WENT WITH SOME OLD FRIENDS TO DANCE. IT WAS ALL DECORATED WITH PALM TREES AND HAD A REAL WATER-FALL AT THE END OF THE ROOM.

ON THE CEILING OF THE PLACE, CLOUDS MOVED AND THERE WERE STARS THAT TWINKLED JUST AS IF THEY WERE REAL.

AND IN EVERY TREE THERE WAS A HUGE STUFFED MONKEY THAT HAD BIG LIGHTS FOR EYES.

I WANT TO BE IN NEW YORK WHERE THERE'S ENOUGH MISCHIEF FOR EVERYBODY—THAT IS, IF I CAN'T BE IN PARIS...THERE'S NOTHING ON EARTH TO DO HERE BUT LOOK AT THE VIEW AND EAT. YOU CAN IMAGINE THE RESULT SINCE I DO NOT LIKE TO LOOK AT VIEWS.

HOW WOULD YOU LIKE TO BE A MOVING PICTURE ACTRESS WHEN YOU ARE A LADY? THEY HAVE PRETTY HOUSES AND LOTS OF MONEY. LAST NIGHT WE WENT TO A HOUSE WAY WAY UP IN THE HILLS AND DOWN BELOW ALL THE LIGHTS OF LOS ANGELES WERE SPREAD OUT LIKE A BEAUTIFUL FIELD OF DAFFODILS.

IN HOLLYWOOD, SCOTT MEETS THE SEVENTEEN-YEAR-OLD ACTRESS LOIS MORAN, AND IS INSTANTLY CHARMED.

LOIS DOES NOT RETURN HIS INFATUATION, BUT THAT DOES NOTHING TO PREVENT THE INEVITABLE QUARREL.

WHAT DOES LOIS HAVE THAT I DON'T?

AT LEAST THE GIRL IS DOING SOMETHING WITH HERSELF!!

INFURIATED, ZELDA BURNS ALL THE CLOTHES SHE'S DESIGNED FOR HERSELF.

AND SHE THROWS THE WATCH SCOTT GAVE HER OUT THE WINDOW OF THE TRAIN.

SCOTT AND ZELDA LEAVE LOS ANGELES.

BACK EAST, ZELDA WANTS A HOUSE ALL HER OWN.

I WANT YOU TO HAVE A LOVELY LITTLE JAPANESE ROOM WITH PINK CHERRY BLOSSOMS AND A DUCKY LITTLE TEA-TABLE AND A SCREEN—WOULD YOU LIKE IT?

AND PERHAPS YOU COULD MAKE A LITTLE GARDEN—I WANT A GARDEN FULL OF LILAC TREES, LIKE PEOPLE HAVE IN FRANCE...

...DADDY SAYS WE MUST RENT A HOUSE FIRST, THO, TO SEE IF WE ARE GOING TO LIKE AMERICA.

THEY CHOOSE A HOUSE, CALLED ELLERSLIE, NEAR WILMINGTON, DELAWARE.

IT'S A LARGE YELLOW HOUSE WITH A COLUMNED PORCH AND VAST MEADOWS RUNNING DOWN TO THE RIVER.

THE SQUARENESS OF THE ROOMS AND THE SWEEP OF THE COLUMNS WERE TO BRING US A JUDICIOUS TRANQUILITY.

THE HOUSE IS TOO LARGE, AND THE FURNITURE SEEMS TO VANISH IN THE ENORMOUS ROOMS.

ZELDA HAS OVERSIZED COUCHES AND CHAIRS MADE TO FILL THE SPACE. BUT WHEN GUESTS SIT ON THEM, THEY LOOK LILLIPUTIAN.

SCOTT AND ZELDA EXTEND AN INVITATION TO THEIR ARTIST FRIENDS TO SPEND LONG WEEKENDS AT ELLERSLIE.

SHE'S REALLY RADIANT, REALLY RADIANT.

THOSE DELIRIOUS PARTIES OF THEIRS; ONE DREADED GOING. AT WILMINGTON, FOR INSTANCE, DINNER WAS NEVER SERVED. OH, A COMPLETE MESS.

JOHN DOS PASSOS

SHE'S SHOWING OFF.

WELL, THEN, SO WAS CHRIST.

WE HAVEN'T GOT ANY MORE GIN.

WILL YOU HAVE A BROMIDE?

THE AFTERMATH OF A FITZGERALD EVENING WAS NOTORIOUSLY A PAINFUL EXPERIENCE.

EDMUND WILSON

113

ON MONDAYS, LIFE AT ELLERSLIE GOES BACK TO NORMAL.

WE GOT TWO DOGS OUT OF THE POUND. ONE OF THEM IS SPLOTCHY BUT MOSTLY WHITE WITH WHISKERS ALTHOUGH HE IS SICK NOW, SO HIS NAME IS EZRA POUND. THE OTHER IS NAMED BOUILLABAISSE, OR MUDDY WATER OR JERRY.

HE DOESN'T ANSWER TO ANY OF THEM SO IT DOESN'T MATTER.

IN MIDSUMMER, ZELDA RESUMES HER DANCE LESSONS, WITH THE PHILADELPHIA OPERA BALLET.

TO BE A PAVLOVA, NOTHING LESS.

THE HEAD OF THE DANCE SCHOOL IS CATHERINE LITTLEFIELD, A PUPIL OF MADAME LUBOV EGOROVA, WHO IS THE DIRECTOR OF SERGEI DIAGHILEV'S BALLET SCHOOL.

ZELDA BUYS A LARGE, ORNATE GILT MIRROR, FROM THE NINETEENTH CENTURY, FOR THE FRONT ROOM. AND WITH THE ADDITION OF A BARRE AND A PHONOGRAPH, SHE PRACTICES THERE ALL DAY.

I SPEND THREE HOURS A DAY PRACTICING MY BALLET ROUTINES TO THE TUNE OF THE "PARADE OF THE WOODEN SOLDIERS."

WHEN SHE'S NOT DANCING, SHE PAINTS...

...AND BUILDS A DOLLHOUSE FOR SCOTTIE.

SHE IS INCREASINGLY DISTANT FROM SCOTT.

BROUGHT UP IN APARTMENT HOTELS AND MARRIED AT THE BEGINNING OF THE DELICATESSEN AGE, ZELDA HAS NOT LEARNED TO COOK ANYTHING SAVE A STRANGE FLUID THAT IN EMERGENCIES SHE EVOLVES FROM THE COFFEE BEAN; SHE IS MOST FAMILIAR WITH THE PRODUCT OF THE SOIL... IN SUCH HIGHLY EVOLVED FORMS...

...AS "TRIPLE COMBINATION SANDWICHES."

YOU ARE CONSTANTLY DRUNK. YOU DON'T WORK AND ARE DRAGGED HOME AT NIGHT BY TAXI-DRIVERS WHEN YOU COME HOME AT ALL. YOU SAY IT IS MY FAULT FOR DANCING ALL DAY. WHAT AM I TO DO?

115

I GOT ANOTHER IDEA FOR A NOVEL GOING THROUGH MY HEAD. HAVE A LOT OF IT WRITTEN UP.

HENRY LOUIS MENCKEN

IT'S ABOUT A WOMAN WHO WANTS TO DESTROY A MAN, BECAUSE SHE LOVES HIM TOO MUCH AND IS AFRAID SHE'LL LOSE HIM, BUT NOT TO ANOTHER WOMAN—BUT BECAUSE SHE'LL STOP LOVING HIM SO MUCH. WELL, SHE DECIDES TO DESTROY HIM BY MARRYING HIM.

SHE MARRIES HIM, AND GETS TO LOVE HIM EVEN MORE THAN SHE DID BEFORE. THEN SHE GETS JEALOUS OF HIM, BECAUSE OF HIS ACHIEVEMENTS IN SOME LINE THAT SHE THINKS SHE'S ALSO GOOD IN.

THEN, I GUESS, SHE COMMITS SUICIDE— FIRST SHE DOES IT STEP BY STEP, THE WAY ALL PEOPLE, ALL WOMEN, COMMIT SUICIDE, BY DRINKING, BY SLEEPING AROUND, BY BEING IMPOLITE TO FRIENDS, AND THAT WAY.

I HAVEN'T GOT THE REST OF IT CLEAR IN MY HEAD, BUT THAT'S THE HEART OF IT.

WHAT DO YOU THINK, HENRY?

116

WELL, IT'S YOUR WIFE, ZELDA, ALL OVER AGAIN.

BUT ZELDA REMAINS HIS MUSE.

11.

BALLET AND DELIRIUM

IN APRIL 1928, SCOTT AND ZELDA RETURN TO PARIS.

WE WERE ON OUR WAY TO PARIS. WE HADN'T MUCH FAITH IN TRAVEL NOR A GREAT BELIEF IN A CHANGE OF SCENE AS A PANACEA FOR SPIRITUAL ILLS; WE WERE SIMPLY GLAD TO BE GOING.

SCOTT MEETS JAMES JOYCE AT A DINNER HELD BY SYLVIA BEACH.

ZELDA MEETS MADAME LUBOV EGOROVA.

ENCHANTED, SHE WATCHES GEORGE BALANCHINE'S LA CHATTE.

OH SCOTT, I WOULD KNOW WHEN I COULD LISTEN WITH MY ARMS AND SEE WITH MY FEET

118

I WANT TO BE A BALLET DANCER.

YOU ARE TOO OLD... WHY HAVE YOU COME TO ME SO LATE?

I DIDN'T KNOW BEFORE. I WAS TOO BUSY LIVING.

CAFÉ de la Ville

AND NOW YOU HAVE DONE ALL YOUR LIVING?

ENOUGH TO BE FED UP.

I DANCE FOR DRIVING THE DEVILS THAT HAVE DRIVEN ME.

I DANCE FOR—IN PROVING MYSELF—ACHIEVING THAT PEACE WHICH I IMAGINE GOES ONLY IN SURETY OF ONE'S SELF.

I DANCE FOR BEING ABLE TO COMMAND MY EMOTIONS, TO SUMMON LOVE OR PITY OR HAPPINESS AT WILL, HAVING PROVIDED A CHANNEL THROUGH WHICH THEY MIGHT FLOW.

DO NOT TOUCH THE LOOKING GLASS

119

WHY WILL YOU NEVER COME OUT WITH ME?

BECAUSE I CAN'T WORK NEXT DAY IF I DO.

ARE YOU UNDER THE ILLUSION THAT YOU'LL EVER BE ANY GOOD AT THAT STUFF?

I SUPPOSE NOT; BUT THERE'S ONLY ONE WAY TO TRY.

YOU'RE HOME ALL DAY BUT IT'S AS IF I WASN'T THERE.

WE HAVE NO LIFE AT HOME ANY MORE.

YOU'RE NEVER THERE ANYWAY— I'VE GOT TO HAVE SOMETHING TO DO WITH MYSELF.

120

YOU WILL TELL ME WHEN I DO WELL ENOUGH TO BUY MYSELF A TUTU?

WHY NOT NOW?

I'D LIKE TO BE A FINE DANCER FIRST.

YOU MUST WORK.

I WORK FOUR HOURS A DAY.

IT IS TOO MUCH.

THEN HOW CAN I BE A DANCER?

I DO NOT KNOW HOW ANYBODY CAN BE ANYTHING.

I WILL BURN CANDLES TO ST. JOSEPH.

PERHAPS THAT WILL HELP; A RUSSIAN SAINT WOULD BE BETTER.

121

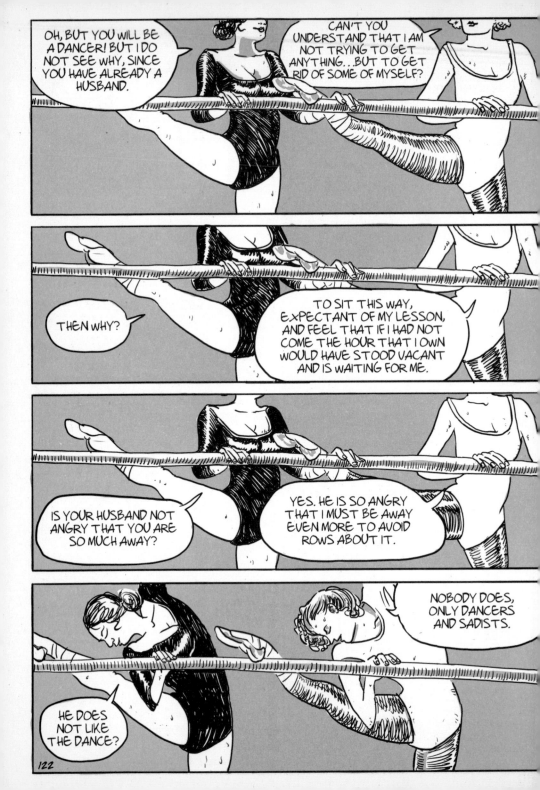

OH, BUT YOU WILL BE A DANCER! BUT I DO NOT SEE WHY, SINCE YOU HAVE ALREADY A HUSBAND.

CAN'T YOU UNDERSTAND THAT I AM NOT TRYING TO GET ANYTHING...BUT TO GET RID OF SOME OF MYSELF?

THEN WHY?

TO SIT THIS WAY, EXPECTANT OF MY LESSON, AND FEEL THAT IF I HAD NOT COME THE HOUR THAT I OWN WOULD HAVE STOOD VACANT AND IS WAITING FOR ME.

IS YOUR HUSBAND NOT ANGRY THAT YOU ARE SO MUCH AWAY?

YES. HE IS SO ANGRY THAT I MUST BE AWAY EVEN MORE TO AVOID ROWS ABOUT IT.

NOBODY DOES, ONLY DANCERS AND SADISTS.

HE DOES NOT LIKE THE DANCE?

122

ZELDA INVITES THE MURPHYS TO A BALLET LESSON.

IT WAS REALLY TERRIBLE...THANK GOD, SHE COULDN'T SEE WHAT SHE LOOKED LIKE.

YOU WILL DANCE ALSO WHEN YOU ARE BIGGER?

NO, IT IS TOO SÉRIEUSE TO BE THE WAY MUMMY IS. SHE WAS NICER BEFORE.

123

IN THE FALL, THE FITZGERALDS ARE AT ELLERSLIE...

...AND ZELDA RESUMES HER STUDIES WITH THE PHILADELPHIA OPERA BALLET...

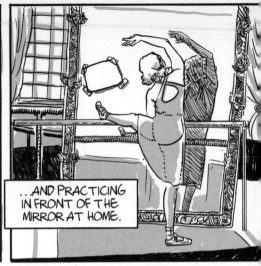

...AND PRACTICING IN FRONT OF THE MIRROR AT HOME.

THEY HIRE PHILIPPE, A PARIS TAXI-DRIVER AND EX-BOXER, TO BE THEIR CHAUFFEUR...

...AND MADEMOISELLE, SCOTTIE'S FRENCH GOVERNESS.

ZELDA DETESTS THEM BOTH.

HOME LIFE HERE IS SIMPLY THE EXISTENCE OF TWO INDIVIDUALS WHO LIVE SIDE BY SIDE, BUT WITHOUT A FOUNDATION OF SHARED INTERESTS.

IN THE SPRING, THEY'RE BACK IN PARIS FOR THE THOUSANDTH TIME, AND ZELDA STUDIES DANCE WITH MADAME EGOROVA. CLASS LESSONS IN THE MORNING...

...AND A PRIVATE LESSON IN THE AFTERNOON.

124

ZELDA WRITES SHORT STORIES TO PAY FOR HER DANCE LESSONS...

I HATED TAKING HIS MONEY FOR MY LESSONS: I WANTED MY DANCING TO BELONG TO ME.

...AND SCOTT EDITS THEM, PUBLISHING THEM UNDER JOINT SIGNATURES.

AT NIGHT, THEY GO ON SOCIALIZING AT MAXIM'S OR LA COUPOLE, WITH KIKI AND DOLLY WILDE, OSCAR WILDE'S NIECE.

NOBODY KNEW WHOSE PARTY IT WAS. IT HAD BEEN GOING ON FOR WEEKS. WHEN YOU FELT YOU COULDN'T SURVIVE ANOTHER NIGHT...A NEW SET OF PEOPLE HAD CONSECRATED THEMSELVES TO KEEPING IT ALIVE.

IN JULY, THEY'RE ON THE COTE D'AZUR.

BY 1929, AT THE MOST GORGEOUS PARADISE FOR SWIMMERS ON THE MEDITERRANEAN NO ONE SWAM ANY MORE, SAVE FOR A SHORT HANGOVER DIP AT NOON.

AND IN SEPTEMBER, THEY'RE IN NAPLES, WHERE ZELDA IS INVITED TO DEBUT WITH A SOLO ROLE IN THE SAN CARLO OPERA BALLET COMPANY, BUT SHE TURNS IT DOWN.

THEY DRIVE BACK TO PARIS IN THE FALL.

ON THE TRIP BACK, ZELDA GRABS THE STEERING WHEEL OF THEIR CAR AND TRIES TO PUT THEM OFF A CLIFF.

125

IS THAT WHY YOU DID IT?

IT'S GONNA GET IN THE PAPERS?

TO GET INTO PRINT?

I GUESS IT WAS SILLY AND STUPID, BUT IT WAS FUN.

WAS IT?

WELL, ALMOST FUN— ON THE VERGE OF BEING FUN.

ONLY IT NEVER QUITE IS, IS IT?

NO...SOMEHOW IT NEVER IS. I DON'T KNOW WHY. MAYBE IT'S SOMETHING ABOUT PARIS OR ME OR THE TIMES OR SOMETHING.

...ONLY YOU NEVER DO.

IT'S AS IF YOU'VE GOT TO HURRY UP, HURRY BEFORE... IT'S LIKE YOU'RE TRYING TO FIND SOMETHING TERRIBLY IMPORTANT, ONLY...

SO I WENT ON AND ON, DANCING ALONE, AND NO MATTER WHAT HAPPENS, I STILL KNOW IN MY HEART THAT IT IS A GODLESS, DIRTY GAME...

...THAT LOVE IS BITTER AND ALL THERE IS, AND THAT THE REST IS FOR THE EMOTIONAL BEGGARS OF THE EARTH AND IS ABOUT THE EQUIVALENT OF PEOPLE WHO STIMULATE THEMSELVES WITH DIRTY POST-CARDS.

126

12.

FIRST HOSPITALIZATIONS

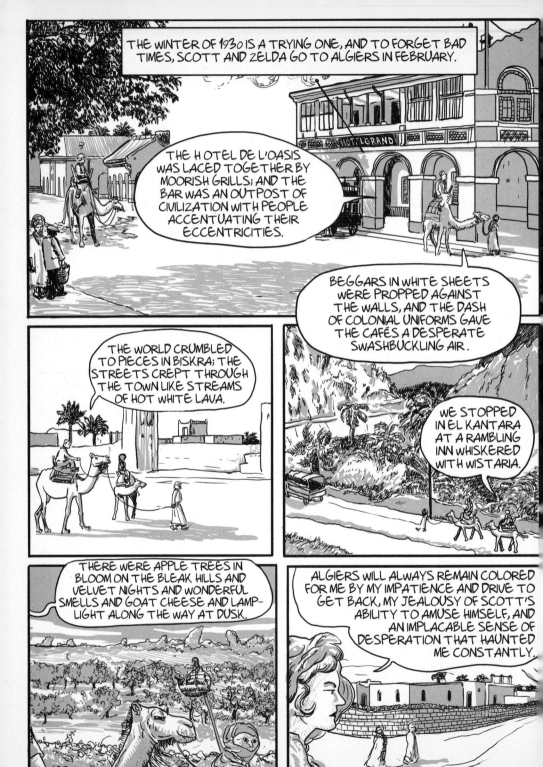

THE WINTER OF 1930 IS A TRYING ONE, AND TO FORGET BAD TIMES, SCOTT AND ZELDA GO TO ALGIERS IN FEBRUARY.

THE HOTEL DE L'OASIS WAS LACED TOGETHER BY MOORISH GRILLS; AND THE BAR WAS AN OUTPOST OF CIVILIZATION WITH PEOPLE ACCENTUATING THEIR ECCENTRICITIES.

BEGGARS IN WHITE SHEETS WERE PROPPED AGAINST THE WALLS, AND THE DASH OF COLONIAL UNIFORMS GAVE THE CAFÉS A DESPERATE SWASHBUCKLING AIR.

THE WORLD CRUMBLED TO PIECES IN BISKRA; THE STREETS CREPT THROUGH THE TOWN LIKE STREAMS OF HOT WHITE LAVA.

WE STOPPED IN EL KANTARA AT A RAMBLING INN WHISKERED WITH WISTARIA.

THERE WERE APPLE TREES IN BLOOM ON THE BLEAK HILLS AND VELVET NIGHTS AND WONDERFUL SMELLS AND GOAT CHEESE AND LAMP-LIGHT ALONG THE WAY AT DUSK.

ALGIERS WILL ALWAYS REMAIN COLORED FOR ME BY MY IMPATIENCE AND DRIVE TO GET BACK, MY JEALOUSY OF SCOTT'S ABILITY TO AMUSE HIMSELF, AND AN IMPLACABLE SENSE OF DESPERATION THAT HAUNTED ME CONSTANTLY.

128

ON THE RETURN FROM ALGERIA, ZELDA FALLS PREY TO HER OBSESSIONS. ON APRIL 23, 1930, ZELDA ENTERS A HOSPITAL, CALLED MALMAISON, ON THE OUTSKIRTS OF PARIS.

IT'S DREADFUL, IT'S HORRIBLE, WHAT'S TO BECOME OF ME, I MUST WORK AND I WON'T BE ABLE TO, I SHOULD DIE, BUT I MUST WORK.

I'LL NEVER BE CURED. LET ME LEAVE.

SHE'S AN ANXIOUS GIRL, EXHAUSTED FROM THE GRUELING EXERCISE IN THE COMPANY OF PROFESSIONAL BALLERINAS.

SHE HAS A NUMBER OF OBSESSIONS. THE MOST FREQUENTLY RECURRING ONE IS THE FEAR OF BECOMING A HOMOSEXUAL...

...SHE'S CONVINCED SHE'S FALLEN IN LOVE WITH HER DANCE TEACHER.

SHE HAS VIOLENT REACTIONS AND HALLUCINATIONS, AND SHE HAS ATTEMPTED SUICIDE REPEATEDLY, ALWAYS PULLING BACK AT THE LAST MINUTE.

ON MAY 2, SHE LEAVES THE CLINIC, AGAINST THE ADVICE OF THE DOCTOR TREATING HER. SHE RESUMES HER DANCE LESSONS AND SOCIALIZING. BUT HER HALLUCINATIONS CONTINUE, AND SO DO THE SUICIDE ATTEMPTS.

ON MAY 22, SHE IS HOSPITALIZED AT THE VALMONT CLINIC IN GLION, SWITZERLAND. BUT IT'S A CLINIC THAT TREATS GASTRO-INTESTINAL CONDITIONS.

DR. OSCAR FOREL IS SUMMONED TO EXAMINE HER. HE DIAGNOSES SCHIZOPHRENIA AND SAYS HE'S WILLING TO ADMIT HER TO HIS CLINIC.

WHAT ROLE DID HER CHILD PLAY IN HER LIFE?

THAT IS DONE NOW, I WANT TO DO SOMETHING ELSE.

I HAD MADE A DECISION: TO ABANDON THE BALLET AND LIVE QUIETLY WITH MY HUSBAND.

ON JUNE 4, ZELDA LEAVES VALMONT AND TRAVELS THROUGH SWITZERLAND WITH SCOTT.

ON JUNE 5, SHE IS ADMITTED TO DR. FOREL'S CLINIC, LES RIVES DES PRANGINS, NEAR NYON, ON THE SHORE OF LAKE GENEVA.

SCOTT IS ONLY ALLOWED TO VISIT HER EVERY TWO OR THREE WEEKS.

IF I COULD NOT SEE HER, COULD I HAVE FLOWERS SENT TO HER EVERY OTHER DAY?

I HAVE THE TERRIBLE MISFORTUNE TO BE A GENTLEMAN IN THE SORT OF STRUGGLE WITH INCALCULABLE ELEMENTS TO WHICH PEOPLE SHOULD BRING CENTURIES OF INEXPERIENCE; IF I HAVE FAILED YOU IS IT JUST BARELY POSSIBLE THAT YOU HAVE FAILED ME...

FLOWERS EVERY OTHER DAY AND LETTERS EVERY DAY—FROM SCOTT TO ZELDA AND FROM ZELDA TO SCOTT.

...I LOVE YOU WITH ALL MY HEART BECAUSE YOU ARE MY OWN GIRL AND THAT IS ALL I KNOW.

SOMETIMES, IT'S DESPERATE TO BE SO ALONE—AND YOU CAN'T BE VERY HAPPY IN A HOTEL ROOM—WE WERE AWFULLY USED TO HAVING EACH OTHER ABOUT.

BUT YOU WERE SICK AND THE HAPPINESS WAS NOT IN THE HOME.

I AM WAITING IMPATIENTLY FOR WHEN YOU CAN COME TO SEE ME IF YOU WILL—DO YOU STILL SMELL OF PENCILS AND SOMETIMES OF TWEED?

LIFE IS PROGRESSIVE, NO MATTER WHAT OUR INTENTIONS, BUT SOMETHING WAS HARMED, SOME PRECEDENT OF POSSIBLE NON-AGREEMENT WAS SET. IT WAS A LOVE MATCH, THOUGH, AND IT COULD STAND A GREAT DEAL.

WHY DID WE LOSE PEACE AND LOVE AND HEALTH, ONE AFTER THE OTHER? IF WE KNEW, IF THERE WAS ANYBODY TO TELL US, I BELIEVE WE COULD TRY.

I'D TRY SO HARD.

ZELDA WANTS TO GET BETTER, BUT SHE SHOWS NO IMPROVEMENT. HER CONDITION IS AGGRAVATED BY A FORM OF ECZEMA THAT COVERS HER NECK, FACE, AND SHOULDERS.

WHERE ARE ALL MY THINGS? I USED TO ALWAYS HAVE DOZENS OF THINGS AND NOW THERE DOESN'T SEEM TO BE ANY CLOTHES OR ANYTHING PERSONAL IN MY TRUNK. I'D LOVE THE GRAMOPHONE.

I CAN'T READ OR SLEEP. WITHOUT HOPE OR YOUTH OR MONEY I SIT CONSTANTLY WISHING I WERE DEAD.

THE WORLD IS UNSTABLE AND VACILLATING... FOR MONTHS I HAVE BEEN LIVING IN VAPOROUS PLACES PEOPLED WITH ONE-DIMENSIONAL FIGURES AND TREMULOUS BUILDINGS UNTIL I CAN NO LONGER TELL AN OPTICAL ILLUSION FROM A REALITY—THAT HEAD AND EARS INCESSANTLY THROB AND ROADS DISAPPEAR, UNTIL FINALLY I LOST ALL CONTROL AND POWERS OF JUDGMENT.

AND THEN I'M RATHER ANGRY BECAUSE PEOPLE WON'T LET ME BE INSANE.

133

ALL THAT SURVIVES IS HER LOVE FOR SCOTT.

DEAREST, MY DARLING, LIVING IS COLD AND TECHNICAL WITHOUT YOU, A DEATH MASK OF ITSELF.

AT SEVEN 'OCLOCK I HAD A BATH BUT YOU WERE NOT IN THE NEXT ROOM TO MAKE IT A BAPTISME OF ALL I WAS THINKING.

AT EIGHT 'OCLOCK I WENT TO GYMNASTICS BUT YOU WERE NOT THERE TO TURN MOVING INTO A HARVESTING OF BREEZES.

AT NINE 'OCLOCK I WENT TO THE TISSAGE AND AN OLD MAN IN A WHITE SMOCK CHANTED INCANTATIONS BUT YOU WERE NOT THERE TO MAKE HIS IMPLORING VOICE SEEM RELIGIOUS.

ALL AFTERNOON I'VE BEEN WRITING SOGGY WORDS IN THE RAIN AND FEELING DANK INSIDE, AND THINKING OF YOU... P.S. SEND THE PHONOGRAPH PLEASE.

AT NOON I PLAYED BRIDGE AND WATCHED DR. FOREL'S PROFILE DISSECTING THE SKY, CONTRE JOUR.

IN NOVEMBER, SHE HAS A RELAPSE AND IS TRANSFERRED BACK TO THE CLINIC. DR. FOREL AND SCOTT CALL IN PAUL EUGEN BLEULER, A LEADING AUTHORITY IN EUROPE IN THE FIELD OF PSYCHIATRY, FOR A CONSULTATION.

SHE IS NEITHER A PURE NEUROSIS NOR A REAL PSYCHOSIS— I CONSIDER HER A CONSTITUTIONAL, EMOTIONALLY UNBALANCED PSYCHOPATH...

...SHE MAY IMPROVE, NEVER COMPLETELY RECOVER.

I WOULD HAVE PREFERRED CARL GUSTAV JUNG, BUT JUNG'S SPECIALTY IS NEUROSIS RATHER THAN PSYCHOSIS. AND AFTER ALL, DR. BLEULER ACTUALLY COINED THE TERM SCHIZOPHRENIA.

BLEULER MEETS ZELDA...

AS THE KING OF GREECE ONCE TOLD ERNEST HEMINGWAY: TO SAVE ONESELF IS THE MOST IMPORTANT THING OF ALL.

...AND GIVES SCOTT HIS DIAGNOSIS.

THREE OUT OF FOUR CASES SUCH AS ZELDA'S WERE DISCHARGED AS CURED... AND THE FOURTH CASE TO GO RIGHT DOWN HILL INTO TOTAL INSANITY... STOP BLAMING YOURSELF. YOU MIGHT HAVE RETARDED IT BUT YOU COULDN'T HAVE PREVENTED IT.

ZELDA FEELS BETTER AND GOES SKIING AT SAINT-CERGUE.

A NEUROSE IS NOT MUCH GOOD IN TIMES OF DISTRESS TO OTHERS.

IN JANUARY, SCOTT'S FATHER DIES, AND SCOTT RETURNS TO AMERICA.

135

IN THE SPRING, ZELDA SEEMS MUCH IMPROVED.

DEAR SCOTT, I WOULD LIKE AWFULLY TO HAVE SOMETHING TO READ... I HAVE BEEN READING JOYCE AND FIND IT A NIGHT-MARE IN MY PRESENT CONDITION—NOT LAWRENCE AND NOT VIRGINIA WOOLF OR ANYBODY WHO WRITES BY DIPPING THE BROKEN THREADS OF THEIR HEADS INTO THE INK OF LITERARY HISTORY, PLEASE.

SHE AND SCOTT MEET IN GENEVA OR LAUSANNE. THEY GO SHOPPING AND EAT IN PASTRY SHOPS, DINING ON CUPS OF HOT CHOCOLATE AND APRICOT TARTS WITH WHIPPED CREAM.

THEY SPEND AN IDYLLIC FORTNIGHT IN ANNECY, PLAYING TENNIS, FISHING, AND DANCING THE WARM EVENINGS AWAY ON THE SHORE OF THE LAKE. HERE, THEY CELEBRATE ZELDA'S THIRTY-FIRST BIRTHDAY.

IT WAS LIKE THE GOOD GONE TIMES WHEN WE STILL BELIEVED IN SUMMER HOTELS AND THE PHILOSOPHIES OF POPULAR SONGS.

ANNECY IS SO BLUE,

ON SEPTEMBER 15, 1931, ZELDA IS RELEASED FROM PRANGINS. SHE AND SCOTT DRIVE TO PARIS TOGETHER, AND FROM THERE, THEY TAKE THE *AQUITANIA* BACK TO THE UNITED STATES.

136

13.

SAVE ME THE WALTZ
VS.
TENDER IS THE NIGHT

IN SEPTEMBER 1931, SCOTT, ZELDA, AND SCOTTIE MOVE TO MONTGOMERY, TAKING A GIGANTIC HOUSE AT 819 FELDER AVENUE. THEY ACQUIRE A SECONDHAND STUTZ AND A COUPLE OF PETS: CHOPIN, A PERSIAN CAT, AND TROUBLE, A BLOODHOUND.

THE PACE OF THEIR DAYS SLOWS DOWN TO MAKING SOCIAL CALLS AND PLAYING SPORTS.

WHAT A MONOTONOUS LIFE.

SCOTT MOVES TO HOLLYWOOD TO WORK AS A SCREENWRITER.

IT'S SUCH A NOTHINGNESS WITHOUT SCOTT.

ZELDA WORKS FOR A LOCAL SCHOOL OF DANCE, WRITES SEVEN STORIES, AND BEGINS PLANNING A NOVEL. OF THE SEVEN STORIES, ONLY ONE IS PUBLISHED.

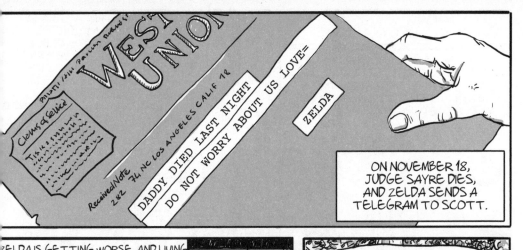

WESTERN UNION

DADDY DIED LAST NIGHT
DO NOT WORRY ABOUT US LOVE=

ZELDA

ON NOVEMBER 18, JUDGE SAYRE DIES, AND ZELDA SENDS A TELEGRAM TO SCOTT.

ZELDA IS GETTING WORSE, AND LIVING WITH HER SISTERS ISN'T HELPING.

YOU AND SCOTT ARE LUCKY.

YOU HAVE AN EASY TIME.

WE GREW UP FOUNDING OUR DREAMS ON THE INFINITE PROMISE OF AMERICAN ADVERTISING. I STILL BELIEVE THAT ONE CAN LEARN TO PLAY THE PIANO BY MAIL AND THAT MUD WILL GIVE YOU A PERFECT COMPLEXION.

I MISS MY DADDY HORRIBLY. I AM LOSING MY IDENTITY HERE WITHOUT MEN. WHERE THERE ARE NONE, THE FIRST THING THAT GOES IS CONCISION.

AT CHRISTMAS, SCOTT COMES HOME, AND HE AND ZELDA TAKE A VACATION IN FLORIDA. THAT IS TO BE THEIR LAST HAPPY VACATION.

139

IN JANUARY 1932, SCOTT STARTS WRITING A NOVEL.

THE HEROINE WAS BORN IN 1901. SHE IS BEAUTIFUL...WIDELY READ BUT WITH NO EXPERIENCE AND NO ORIENTATION EXCEPT WHAT HE SUPPLIES HER. PORTRAIT OF ZELDA THAT IS, A PART OF ZELDA.

IN FEBRUARY, ZELDA HAS A RELAPSE AND IS COMMITTED TO THE HENRY PHIPPS PSYCHIATRIC CLINIC IN BALTIMORE. UNDER THE CARE OF DOCTORS ADOLF MEYER AND MILDRED SQUIRES, SHE STAYS THERE FOR THREE MONTHS AND, WORKING NO MORE THAN TWO HOURS A DAY, WRITES HER NOVEL.

I HAVE CAT THOUGHTS THAT CHASE THE MOUSE THOUGHTS AND SOMETIMES THEY WILL GET ALL THE MOUSE THOUGHTS CAUGHT...

...AND I READ AESCHYLUS TO PUT MYSELF TO SLEEP.

I'M SURE MY FAMILY SECRETLY THINKS THAT SCOTT'S THE CRAZY ONE: THEY'VE READ STORIES LIKE THAT, ABOUT INCARCERATED WIVES.

ANYWAY, THERE'S NOTHING SO SORDID AS BEING SHUT UP.

SCOTT TAKES SCOTTIE DANCING. HE MISSES ZELDA.

THAT'S SCOTT FITZGERALD WITH HIS LITTLE GIRL.

PERHAPS 50 PERCENT OF OUR FRIENDS AND RELATIVES WOULD TELL YOU IN ALL HONEST CONVICTION THAT MY DRINKING DROVE ZELDA INSANE—THE OTHER HALF WOULD ASSURE YOU THAT HER INSANITY DROVE ME TO DRINK.

NEITHER JUDGMENT WOULD MEAN ANYTHING.

LIQUOR ON MY MOUTH IS SWEET TO HER; I CHERISH HER MOST EXTRAVAGANT HALLUCINATIONS.

140

IN SIX WEEKS, ZELDA FINISHES HER NOVEL, AND IN MARCH, WITHOUT INFORMING SCOTT, SHE SENDS IT TO MAXWELL PERKINS AT SCRIBNER'S. SCOTT RECEIVES THE NOVEL FROM PERKINS AND IS FURIOUS.

ONE WHOLE SECTION OF HER NOVEL IS AN IMITATION OF IT, OF ITS RHYTHM, MATERIALS, EVEN STATEMENTS AND SPEECHES.

THE NOVEL CAUSES FRESH DIVISIONS BETWEEN THEM.

OF COURSE, I GLADLY SUBMIT TO ANYTHING YOU WANT ABOUT THE BOOK OR ANYTHING ELSE... HOWEVER, I WOULD LIKE YOU TO THOROUGHLY UNDERSTAND THAT MY REVISION WILL BE MADE ON AN AESTHETIC BASIS.

SCOTT MOVES TO BALTIMORE AND WORKS WITH ZELDA ON THE EDITING OF THE MANUSCRIPT.

THERE ARE GOOD IDEAS FOR TITLES IN THE VICTOR RECORD CATALOGUE: "SAVE ME THE WALTZ," FOR INSTANCE.

IT IS A GOOD NOVEL NOW, PERHAPS A VERY GOOD NOVEL—I AM TOO CLOSE TO TELL. IT HAS THE FAULTS AND VIRTUES OF A FIRST NOVEL.

IN MAY, SCOTT RENTS A COTTAGE, CALLED LA PAIX, IN A BALTIMORE SUBURB. ZELDA IS ABLE TO MOVE THERE IN JUNE.

IN THIS VERY POLITE MARYLAND ATMOSPHERE...SCOTT READS MARX—I READ THE COSMOLOGICAL PHILOSOPHERS. THE BRIGHTEST MOMENTS OF OUR DAY ARE WHEN WE GET THEM MIXED UP.

141

SAVE ME THE WALTZ

HERE IS A PECULIAR TALENT, AND CONNOISSEURS OF STYLE WILL HAVE A WONDERFUL TIME WITH *SAVE ME THE WALTZ*...PASSAGES GIVE THE BOOK AN ALMOST ALCOHOLIC VITALITY.

THE NEW YORK TIMES

THE SUN

ON OCTOBER 7, 1932, *SAVE ME THE WALTZ* IS PUBLISHED WITH A PRINT RUN OF LESS THAN 3,000 COPIES, SELLING ONLY 1,392 COPIES. ZELDA EARNS ROYALTIES OF $120.73 FROM THE NOVEL. THE REVIEWS ARE NOT ENTIRELY POSITIVE, AND THE BOOK IS A COMMERCIAL FAILURE.

IT IS NOT ONLY THAT HER PUBLISHERS HAVE NOT SEEN FIT TO CURB AN ALMOST LUDICROUS LUSHNESS OF WRITING BUT THEY HAVE NOT GIVEN THE BOOK THE ELEMENTARY SERVICES OF A LITERATE PROOFREADER.

SCOTT DRINKS AND QUARRELS MORE AND MORE WITH ZELDA. HE TOO STARTS GOING TO PHIPPS FOR THERAPY.

FAMILY QUARRELS ARE BITTER THINGS. THEY DON'T GO ACCORDING TO ANY RULES. THEY'RE NOT LIKE ACHES OR WOUNDS; THEY'RE MORE LIKE SPLITS IN THE SKIN THAT WON'T HEAL BECAUSE THERE'S NOT ENOUGH MATERIAL.

I CANNOT CONSIDER ONE PINT OF WINE AT THE DAY'S END AS ANYTHING BUT ONE OF THE RIGHTS OF MAN.

THERE'S A JAPANESE PROVERB THAT SAYS: FIRST YOU TAKE A DRINK, THEN THE DRINK TAKES A DRINK, THEN THE DRINK TAKES YOU.

142

Panel 1 (caption): SCOTT AND ZELDA TRY TO DISCUSS THEIR PROBLEMS AS A COUPLE WITH DR. RENNIE.

YOU ARE A THIRD-RATE WRITER AND A THIRD-RATE BALLET DANCER.

YOU HAVE TOLD ME THAT BEFORE.

I AM A PROFESSIONAL WRITER, WITH A HUGE FOLLOWING. I AM THE HIGHEST PAID SHORT STORY WRITER IN THE WORLD. I HAVE AT VARIOUS TIMES DOMINATED—

IT SEEMS TO ME YOU ARE MAKING A RATHER VIOLENT ATTACK ON A THIRD RATE TALENT THEN.

Panel 2:

I TELL YOU, MY LIFE HAS BEEN SO MISERABLE THAT I WOULD RATHER BE IN AN ASYLUM. DOES THAT MEAN A THING TO YOU?

IT DOES NOT MEAN A BLESSED THING!

I WANT YOU TO STOP WRITING FICTION.

WHAT DO YOU WANT ME TO DO?

Panel 3:

WHAT IS OUR MARRIAGE ANYWAY? IT HAS BEEN NOTHING BUT A LONG BATTLE EVER SINCE I CAN REMEMBER.

I DON'T KNOW ABOUT THAT. WE WERE ABOUT THE MOST ENVIED COUPLE IN 1921 IN AMERICA.

WE WERE AWFULLY GOOD SHOWMEN.

WE WERE AWFULLY HAPPY.

Panel 4:

YOU HAVE TO STOP WRITING FICTION.

OF ANY KIND?

IF YOU WRITE A PLAY, IT CANNOT BE A PLAY ABOUT PSYCHIATRY, AND IT CANNOT BE A PLAY LAID ON THE RIVIERA, AND IT CANNOT BE A PLAY LAID IN SWITZERLAND, AND WHATEVER THE IDEA IS, IT WILL HAVE TO BE SUBMITTED TO ME.

YOU DON'T LOVE ME—BUT I AM COUNTING ON PAVLOV'S DOGS TO MAKE THAT KIND OF THING ALL RIGHT.

143

ALONE, SCOTT DELVES INTO HIS WIFE'S ILLNESS. HE SPEAKS TO ZELDA, IN AN IMAGINARY CONVERSATION WITH HER.

DO YOU FEEL THAT YOU ARE NOW ABLE TO BE YOUR OWN DOCTOR—TO JUDGE WHAT IS GOOD FOR YOU? IF NO—DO YOU KNOW WHAT SHOULD BE DONE? SHOULD YOU BE IN A CLINIC DO YOU THINK? WOULD A TRAINED NURSE HELP?

IF YOU WERE REALLY NOT YOURSELF AND IN A FIT OF TEMPER OR DEPRESSION WOULD YOU ASK THE JUDGMENT OF SUCH A WOMAN OR WOULD YOU COME TO ME? ARE THESE BURSTS OF TEMPER PART OF THE "DERANGEMENT" YOU MENTIONED? OR ARE THEY SOMETHING THAT IS IN YOUR SURROUNDINGS?

IF YOU FEEL THAT YOU ARE NOW ABLE TO BE YOUR OWN DOCTOR—TO JUDGE WHAT IS GOOD FOR YOU. OF WHAT USE WOULD A NURSE BE?

WOULD SHE BE A SORT OF CLOCK TO REMIND YOU IT WAS TIME FOR THIS AND THAT? IF THAT FUNCTION IN YOUR HUSBAND IS ANNOYING WOULD IT NOT BE MORE ANNOYING IN THE CASE OF A STRANGER IN YOUR OWN HOUSE?

IS THERE NOT AN IDEA IN YOUR IDEA SOMETIMES THAT YOU MUST LIVE CLOSE TO THE BORDERS OF MENTAL TROUBLE IN ORDER TO CREATE AT YOUR BEST?

WHICH COMES FIRST, YOUR HEALTH OR YOUR WORK?

ARE YOU IN DELICATE HEALTH?

DOES FURIOUS ACTIVITY LEAD OFTEN TO CONSEQUENT IRRITABILITY EVEN IN WELL PERSONS? WOULD NOT THIS BE TERRIBLY ACCENTUATED BY AN ILL PERSON? DOES A PERSON RECOVERING FROM HEART TROUBLE START BY MOVING BOULDERS?

WHAT IS THE ORDER OF IMPORTANCE OF EVERYTHING IN YOUR MIND—IS YOUR HEALTH FIRST? IS IT ALWAYS FIRST? IS IT FIRST IN THE MIDST OF ARTISTIC CREATION WHEN THE TWO ARE IN CONFLICT?

WHY DOES MADNESS NOT ENLARGE THE ARTISTIC RANGE?

WHO PAYS FOR ILLNESS? WHO PAYS IN SUFFERING? DOES ONLY THE ILL PERSON SUFFER?

WHEN DOCTORS RECOMMEND A NORMAL SEXUAL LIFE DO YOU AGREE WITH THEM? ARE YOU NORMAL SEXUALLY? ARE YOU RETISCENT ABOUT SEX? ARE YOU SATISFIED SEXUALLY WITH YOUR HUSBAND?

145

IN JUNE 1933, A FIRE BREAKS OUT AT LA PAIX, PROBABLY CAUSED BY ZELDA. THE HOUSE IS SERIOUSLY DAMAGED.

IN AUGUST, ZELDA'S BROTHER, ANTHONY, KILLS HIMSELF BY JUMPING OUT A WINDOW. ZELDA, SCOTT, AND SCOTTIE MOVE TO 1307 PARK AVENUE IN BALTIMORE.

THEY TAKE A TRIP TO BERMUDA, IN HOPES OF DISTRACTION, BUT THE RAIN AND SCOTT'S PLEURISY RUIN THE HOLIDAY.

BERMUDA WAS A NICE PLACE TO BE THE LAST ONE OF SO MANY YEARS OF TRAVELLING.

IN FEBRUARY, ZELDA IS HOSPITALIZED AT THE PHIPPS CLINIC. SHE IS ALARMINGLY SKINNY AND IS THREATENING TO KILL HERSELF.

IN MARCH, SHE IS MOVED TO CRAIG HOUSE, A PRIVATE AND ELEGANT NURSING HOME IN BEACON, NEW YORK, AT A COST OF $175 A WEEK.

BEAUTY ON DISPLAY COSTS MONEY, BUT AS TOLSTOY DISCOVERED LONG BEFORE EINSTEIN ALL THINGS ARE RELATIVE.

AT THE END OF MARCH, SCOTT PUTS TOGETHER TWO SHOWS OF HER ART IN MANHATTAN: ONE AT THE STUDIO OF CARY ROSS, AND THE OTHER AT THE ALGONQUIN HOTEL.

ON APRIL 12, 1934, TENDER IS THE NIGHT IS PUBLISHED. IT CONTAINS WHOLE SENTENCES TAKEN FROM ZELDA'S LETTERS.

THE TITLE IS FROM JOHN KEATS' "ODE TO A NIGHTINGALE": "TENDER IS THE NIGHT, AND HAPLY THE QUEEN-MOON IS ON HER THRONE."

I CAN'T DO ANYTHING FOR YOU ANY MORE. I'M TRYING TO SAVE MYSELF.

FROM MY CONTAMINATION?

14.

MORE HOSPITALIZATIONS

ON MAY 19, 1934, ZELDA IS MOVED TO THE SHEPPARD AND ENOCH PRATT HOSPITAL ON THE OUTSKIRTS OF BALTIMORE, WHERE SHE IS TO REMAIN FOR THE NEXT TWO YEARS. SHE BECOMES INCREASINGLY DEPRESSED AND SUFFERS FROM HALLUCINATIONS. SHE HEARS VOICES COMING FROM THE DRAIN PIPES AND FROM WITHIN HERSELF, AND SHE BELIEVES THEY ARE SCOTT'S.

OH, I HAVE KILLED HER!

I HAVE LOST THE WOMAN I PUT INTO MY BOOK.

PLEASE, PLEASE, DON'T BE IN AN INSANE ASYLUM.

OH, SCOTT...

IN THE MEANTIME, SCOTT TRIES TO HELP HER PUT TOGETHER A COLLECTION OF SHORT STORIES. AND AS SOON AS HE CAN, HE VISITS HER.

YOU SEEM IN EVERY WAY EXACTLY LIKE THE GIRL I USED TO KNOW.

I WISH WE WERE ASTRIDE THE TOPS OF NEW YORK TAXIS AND A LITTLE HILARIOUS IN PARKS AND PUBLIC PLACES...

...AND YOUNGER THAN YOUNG PEOPLE.

ZELDA'S BEHAVIOR VACILLATES BETWEEN ABSOLUTE VIOLENCE AND ABSOLUTE RESERVE. AND SHE NEVER STOPS CRYING.

WHAT'S IT ABOUT?

OH, THAT'S A TABLE IN SPAIN...

...SEEN FROM THE COAST OF THE UNITED STATES.

IN APRIL 1936, SCOTT, WHO HAS NEVER BEEN TO BED WITH ANY GIRL BESIDES ZELDA—AT LEAST UNTIL ZELDA'S INSANITY WAS OFFICIALLY DIAGNOSED—HAS AN AFFAIR WITH BEATRICE DANCE, A YOUNG MARRIED WOMAN FROM SAN ANTONIO. SHE IS STAYING, LIKE HIM, AT THE GROVE PARK INN IN ASHEVILLE. THE AFFAIR LASTS SEVEN WEEKS. SHE IS THE FIRST WOMAN WHO MAKES HIM FORGET ABOUT ZELDA, IF ONLY BRIEFLY.

A FEW MONTHS LATER, THE CRACK-UP STARTS FOR SCOTT.

I ONLY WANTED ABSOLUTE QUIET TO THINK OUT WHY I HAD DEVELOPED A SAD ATTITUDE TOWARDS SADNESS, A MELANCHOLY ATTITUDE TOWARD MELANCHOLY, AND A TRAGIC ATTITUDE TOWARD TRAGEDY— WHY I HAD BECOME IDENTIFIED WITH THE OBJECTS OF MY HORROR OR COMPASSION.

I BEGAN TO REALIZE THAT FOR TWO YEARS MY LIFE HAD BEEN A DRAWING ON RESOURCES THAT I DID NOT POSSESS, THAT I HAD BEEN MORTGAGING MYSELF PHYSICALLY AND SPIRITUALLY UP TO THE HILT.

AND CRACKED LIKE AN OLD PLATE.

SOMETIMES, THOUGH, THE CRACKED PLATE HAS TO BE RETAINED IN THE PANTRY... IT WILL NOT BE BROUGHT OUT FOR COMPANY, BUT IT WILL DO TO HOLD CRACKERS LATE AT NIGHT OR TO GO INTO THE ICEBOX UNDER LEFTOVERS.

ON APRIL 7, 1936 ZELDA LEAVES SHEPPARD-PRATT FOR HIGHLAND HOSPITAL IN ASHEVILLE, WHERE SHE IS PLACED IN THE CARE OF DR. ROBERT S. CARROLL.

I WISH OUR GRAVEST TROUBLES WERE THE SUMMER GNATS. I WISH WE WERE HUNGRY FOR HOT DOGS AND DOPES AND IT WOULD BE NICE TO SMELL THE STARCH OF SUMMER LINENS AND THE FAINT ODOR OF TALC IN BLISTERING BATHHOUSES.

SHE WEIGHS ONLY NINETY POUNDS. OVER THE PREVIOUS THREE MONTHS, IN THE THROES OF AN INTENSE SUICIDAL MANIA, SHE HAS TRIED TO STRANGLE HERSELF AND THROW HERSELF IN FRONT OF A TRAIN.

THIS IS THE BEGINNING OF A LONG PERIOD OF INTENSE RELIGIOUS FERVOR; SHE IS CONVINCED THAT EVERYONE BUT HER IS DESTINED FOR HELL.

ZELDA NOW CLAIMS TO BE IN DIRECT CONTACT WITH CHRIST, WILLIAM THE CONQUEROR, MARY STUART, APOLLO AND ALL THE STOCK PARAPHERNALIA OF INSANE-ASYLUM JOKES.

OUTSIDE OF THE REALM OF WHAT YOU CALLED ZELDA'S "TERRIBLY DANGEROUS SECRET THOUGHTS" I AM HER GREAT REALITY, OFTEN THE ONLY LIAISON AGENT WHO COULD MAKE THE WORLD TANGIBLE TO HER.

YOU ARE HER EMOTIONAL DISORGANIZER.

ONE OF THE THERAPIES USED BY DR. CARROLL IS EXERCISE. HE ASSIGNS EACH PATIENT A DISTANCE FOR CLIMBING UP AND DOWN A HILL, A CERTAIN NUMBER OF TIMES EACH DAY.

TO ACCUSTOM THE PATIENT TO THE REALITY OF ENDEAVOR, ENDLESS AND ROUTINE.

150

THE FOLLOWING JULY, COTT LEAVES BALTIMORE AND RETURNS TO ASHEVILLE'S GROVE PARK INN. BUT HE BREAKS HIS SHOULDER IN A DIVING ACCIDENT IN THE HOTEL SWIMMING POOL.

SOON AFTER, HE SLIPS AND FALLS IN THE BATHROOM AND LIES IMMOBILE ON THE FLOOR, UNABLE TO SUMMON HELP. THIS RESULTS IN A BAD COLD AND AN ATTACK OF ARTHRITIS.

HE HAS A REVOLVER, AND HE USES IT TO ATTEMPT SUICIDE. BUT HE IS UNSUCCESSFUL.

I WAS ON MY BACK FOR TEN WEEKS, WITH WHOLE DAYS IN WHICH I WAS OUT OF BED TRYING TO WRITE OR DICTATE... THE MORE I WORRIED, THE LESS I COULD WRITE.

BEING ONE MILE FROM ZELDA, I SAW HER TWICE ALL SUMMER, AND WAS UNABLE TO GO NORTH WHEN MY MOTHER HAD A STROKE AND DIED.

YOU HAVE PROBABLY GUESSED THAT I HAVE BEEN DOING A GOOD DEAL OF DRINKING.

WE HAVE NOW BEEN MARRIED MOST PORTENTOUSLY SEVENTEEN YEARS, RATHER AN ASTOUNDING ACCUMULATION OF TIME. WE SHOULD HAVE HAD A CAKE.

HE AND ZELDA SEE LESS AND LESS OF EACH OTHER AND WRITE EACH OTHER MORE AND MORE.

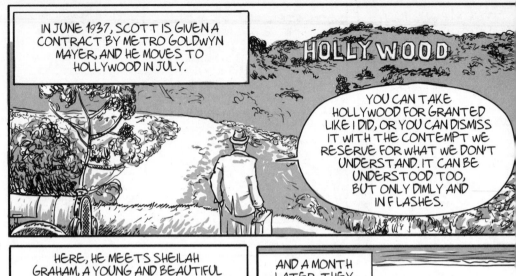

IN JUNE 1937, SCOTT IS GIVEN A CONTRACT BY METRO GOLDWYN MAYER, AND HE MOVES TO HOLLYWOOD IN JULY.

HOLLYWOOD

YOU CAN TAKE HOLLYWOOD FOR GRANTED LIKE I DID, OR YOU CAN DISMISS IT WITH THE CONTEMPT WE RESERVE FOR WHAT WE DON'T UNDERSTAND. IT CAN BE UNDERSTOOD TOO, BUT ONLY DIMLY AND IN FLASHES.

HERE, HE MEETS SHEILAH GRAHAM, A YOUNG AND BEAUTIFUL GOSSIP COLUMNIST, SOMETHING OF A FEMALE GATSBY

SHE REMINDS ME OF ZELDA.

AND A MONTH LATER, THEY BECOME LOVERS.

HOW DIFFERENT EVERYTHING TURNS OUT FROM WHAT ONE PLANS.

STILL, SCOTT NEITHER STOPS LOVING ZELDA, NOR DOES HE ABANDON HER. AT CHRISTMAS HE GOES TO SEE HER IN ASHEVILLE AND TAKES HER TO FLORIDA FOR A VACATION—IN MIAMI AND PALM BEACH—AND FROM THERE, TO MONTGOMERY, TO VISIT HER MOTHER.

SUPPOSING ZELDA AT BEST WOULD BE A LIFELONG ECCENTRIC, SUPPOSING THAT IN TWO OR THREE YEARS THERE IS CERTAIN TO BE A SINKING, I AM STILL HAUNTED BY THE FACT THAT IF IT WERE ME, AND ZELDA WERE PASSING JUDGMENT, I WOULD WANT HER TO GIVE ME A CHANCE.

152

BUT ZELDA ISN'T GETTING BETTER, AND SCOTT KEEPS DRINKING MORE AND MORE.

REASONS FOR DRINKING: ZELDA'S TRAGEDY, MY CONSTANT FINANCIAL WORRIES, MY CONVICTION THAT I AM A FAILURE, MY DISILLUSIONMENT ABOUT THE KINGDOM OF THE VERY RICH...

...AND MY SORROW OVER THE SWIFT PASSING OF YOUTH AND ROMANTIC LOVE.

I HAVE TO DRINK IN ORDER TO WRITE.

IN MARCH 1938, SCOTT, ZELDA, AND SCOTTIE TAKE A VACATION TO VIRGINIA BEACH THAT PROVES TO BE A DISASTER.

I DID NOTHING BUT GET DRUNK, AND SHE TOLD EVERYONE I WAS OUT OF MY MIND.

WE SIMPLY COULD NOT BE IN EACH OTHER'S COMPANY FOR MORE THAN A FEW DAYS AT A TIME.

IN JUNE, ZELDA ATTENDS SCOTTIE'S HIGH SCHOOL GRADUATION IN CONNECTICUT.

IN SEPTEMBER, SCOTTIE SEES ZELDA IN NEW YORK, ALONG WITH ROSALIND, MRS. SAYRE, AND CLOTILDE.

NEW YORK IS BLISS, AGAIN... AND BEING HERE IN A LAND OF SO MUCH PROMISE—AND SO MANY PROMISES—IS TO LIVE IN A DREAM.

153

THE NEXT YEAR, ZELDA STARTS PLANNING A TRIP TO CUBA.

THERE'S CUBA: A BODY OF LAND ENTIRELY SURROUNDED BY WATER ETC. WHY DON'T WE GO THERE?

THEY SET OFF FOR CUBA IN APRIL, BUT SCOTT DRINKS FROM START TO FINISH. WHEN THEY ARRIVE, HE IS BEATEN UP. ZELDA HAS TO TAKE HIM BACK TO NEW YORK AND PUT HIM IN THE HOSPITAL. SHE MUST THEN MAKE HER OWN ARRANGEMENTS TO GET BACK TO HIGHLAND HOSPITAL. IT WILL BE THE LAST TIME SCOTT AND ZELDA EVER SEE EACH OTHER.

DEAR, I'M SORRY THIS TRIP HAS BEEN SO CATASTROPHIC: I'M GRATEFUL FOR THE GENEROSITY OF YOUR INTENT; AND ALWAYS HOPING THAT YOU WILL FEEL BETTER— PRETTY SOON.

BY THE FALL, SCOTT, WHO HAS STARTED WRITING *THE LAST TYCOON*, IS SO DEEP IN DEBT, HE HAS TO ASK DR. CARROLL TO EXTEND CREDIT.

I AM ONLY TOO AWARE HOW MUCH LACK OF MONEY CRIPPLES A PERSON.

IT IS EXTREMELY AWKWARD TO BE WITHOUT MONEY BUT EVEN MORE AWKWARD NOT TO BE ABLE TO FACE THE ISSUE.

ZELDA SPENDS CHRISTMAS IN MONTGOMERY, AND THAT WINTER, SHE PAINTS SCREENS FOR THE ROOMS OF THE PATIENTS AT HIGHLAND HOSPITAL.

DR. CARROLL HAS APPORTIONED ME A JOB WHICH IS OF THE DEEPEST INTEREST, IF OF SOMEWHAT GARGANTUAN PROPORTIONS... THE JOB WILL PROBABLY TAKE YEARS: BUT PAINTING FOR A PUBLIC BUILDING SUCH AS THIS...IS AN AMBITIOUS AND VERY COMPELLING PROJECT.

ON APRIL 25, 1940, ZELDA IS RELEASED. SHE GOES TO LIVE WITH HER MOTHER AT 322 SAYRE STREET, IN A HOUSE NICKNAMED RABBIT RUN.

IT'S WONDERFUL TO BE FREE FROM THOSE SO COMPELLING OBLIGATIONS OF HOSPITAL ROUTINE: IT WOULD SEEM IMPOSSIBLE THAT A PERSON COULD HAVE BEEN SO EXHAUSTED AS I WAS AND STILL SURVIVE.

BY JULY, HER DAYS CONSIST OF GARDENING, VOLUNTEERING AT THE LOCAL RED CROSS, FOLLOWING DR. CARROLL'S EXERCISE REGIMEN, AND SITTING IDLY WITH HER MOTHER ON THE FRONT PORCH, KEEPING COOL. SHE IS BORED.

TO THIS SORT OF TOWN A BEAU IS ALMOST INDISPENSABLE; BUT THERE DON'T SEEM TO BE ANY LEFT.

I DON'T WRITE; AND I DON'T PAINT: LARGELY BECAUSE IT REQUIRES MOST OF MY RESOURCES TO KEEP OUT OF THE HOSPITAL.

SHE AND SCOTT CONTINUE TO WRITE EACH OTHER. AS SOON AS HE IS ABLE, SCOTT SENDS HER MONEY, AND FOR HER FORTIETH BIRTHDAY, HE SENDS A LARGE BOX OF DAHLIAS AND GLADIOLAS.

YOU ARE SO THOUGHTFUL TO REMEMBER THE COSTLINESS OF THE UNUSUAL— AND IN SENDING ME THE MEANS OF MASTERY.

THANKS AGAIN FOR SAVING ME. SOMEDAY, I'LL SAVE YOU TOO.

155

IN NOVEMBER 1940, SCOTT GOES OUT TO BUY A PACK OF CIGARETTES AND SUFFERS A CARDIAC SPASM. BUT HE RECOVERS. ON DECEMBER 20, HE SUFFERS ANOTHER ATTACK, AT THE PANTAGES THEATRE, DURING A PRESS PREVIEW OF THE MOVIE *THIS THING CALLED LOVE*. AGAIN, HE RECOVERS. THE NEXT DAY, HE HAS HIS FINAL HEART ATTACK, AT HOME, WHILE MAKING NOTES ON AN ARTICLE IN THE *PRINCETON ALUMNI WEEKLY* AND EATING A CHOCOLATE BAR.

AND THEN I DIED.

ON DECEMBER 27, SCOTT IS BURIED AT ROCKVILLE UNION CEMETERY IN MARYLAND. ZELDA IS UNABLE TO ATTEND THE FUNERAL. THOSE PRESENT INCLUDE SCOTTIE, GERALD AND SARA MURPHY, MAX PERKINS, HAROLD OBER, JUDGE BIGGS, LUDLOW FOWLER, AND MR. AND MRS. BAYARD TURNBULL.

FRANCIS SCOTT FITZGERALD
September 24, 1892
December 21, 1940

HE IS DENIED A CATHOLIC BURIAL BECAUSE HIS BOOKS ARE CONDEMNED BY THE CHURCH.

WHAT DID HE DIE OF?

HE DIED OF JUS' SHEER DIE-ABILITY.

IN RETROSPECT IT SEEMS AS IF HE WAS ALWAYS PLANNING HAPPINESSES FOR SCOTTIE AND FOR ME. BOOKS TO READ—PLACES TO GO. LIFE SEEMED SO PROMISSORY ALWAYS WHEN HE WAS AROUND: AND I ALWAYS BELIEVED THAT HE COULD TAKE CARE OF ANYTHING.

15.

ZELDA WITHOUT SCOTT

I MISS HIM.

AFTER SCOTT'S DEATH, ZELDA STAYS WITH HER MOTHER IN THE HOUSE ON SAYRE STREET...

AAAAAHHHHH

...A ONCE QUIET STREET, NOW OVERRUN BY CHILDREN AND TAXIS.

IN OCTOBER 1941, *THE LAST TYCOON* IS PUBLISHED, POSTHUMOUSLY.

I'M THE LAST OF THE NOVELISTS FOR A LONG TIME NOW.

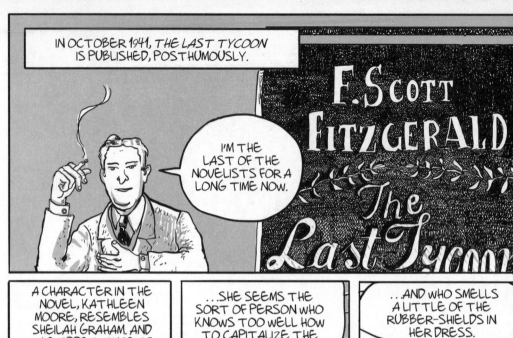

F. SCOTT FITZGERALD
The Last Tycoon

A CHARACTER IN THE NOVEL, KATHLEEN MOORE, RESEMBLES SHEILAH GRAHAM. AND THE APPEARANCE OF ANOTHER MUSE DEEPLY IRRITATES ZELDA.

I CONFESS THAT I DON'T LIKE THE HEROINE...

...SHE SEEMS THE SORT OF PERSON WHO KNOWS TOO WELL HOW TO CAPITALIZE THE UNWELCOME ADVANCES OF THE ICE-MAN...

...AND WHO SMELLS A LITTLE OF THE RUBBER-SHIELDS IN HER DRESS.

160

IN MAY AND DECEMBER OF THE FOLLOWING YEAR, ZELDA'S ARTWORK IS EXHIBITED IN MONTGOMERY, AT THE MUSEUM OF NEW ARTS AND AT THE WOMAN'S CLUB, RESPECTIVELY.

WHILE CONTINUING TO PAINT, SHE STARTS A SECOND AUTOBIOGRAPHICAL NOVEL THAT SHE IS NEVER TO COMPLETE, LEAVING A 135-PAGE MANUSCRIPT.

I AM TRYING TO WRITE A NOVEL WITH THE THEMATIC INTENT OF INDUCTING...

...THE BIBLICAL PATTERN OF LIFE INTO ITS EVERYDAY MANIFESTATIONS.

THE NOVEL WILL BE CALLED *CAESAR'S THINGS*, FOR I HAVE LEARNED TO SEPARATE CAESAR'S THINGS FROM GOD'S.

IN FEBRUARY 1943, SCOTTIE MARRIES LIEUTENANT SAMUEL JACKSON LANAHAN.

ZELDA DOES NOT GO TO THE WEDDING. BUT SCOTTIE DOES SEND HER SOME WEDDING CAKE, WHICH SHE SHARES WITH JOHN DOS PASSOS WHO IS PASSING THROUGH MONTGOMERY.

ZELDA AND SCOTTIE SPEND THEIR SUMMER VACATION IN NEW YORK.

ZELDA STARTS TO SHOW NEW SIGNS OF MENTAL INSTABILITY, AND IN AUGUST, SHE IS BACK IN HIGHLAND HOSPITAL.

IN FEBRUARY 1944, SHE RETURNS TO MONTGOMERY, CONSTANTLY OBSESSED WITH RELIGION. SHE SPENDS HER DAYS WRITING TRACTS AND MAKING COPIES OF THEM FOR HER FRIENDS, TO SAVE THEM.

YOU ARE MUCH TO BE RESPECTED AND HANDSOME AND HAVE A GENIUS FOR INTERESTING PEOPLE. YOU MUST LOOK TO YOUR SALVATION.

IN THE MEANTIME, SCOTT'S ESTATE IS SETTLED, AND ZELDA RECEIVES HALF, OR $15,000; AN ANNUITY WILL PAY HER $50 A MONTH, AND A BANK ACCOUNT IS SET UP IN HER NAME.

SHE SPENDS THE YEARS THAT FOLLOW PAINTING, WRITING, AND, OCCASIONALLY, RELAPSING AND BEING INSTITUTIONALIZED.

WHAT I WANT TO DO IS TO PAINT THE BASIC, FUNDAMENTAL PRINCIPLE SO THAT EVERYONE WILL BE FORCED TO REALIZE AND EXPERIENCE IT...

...I WANT TO PAINT A BALLET STEP SO ALL WILL KNOW WHAT IT IS.

163

ON APRIL 26, 1946, THE FIRST OF SCOTTIE'S FOUR CHILDREN, TIMOTHY, IS BORN.

ZELDA PAINTS BOWLS WITH IMAGES OF THEIR TRAVELS WHEN SCOTTIE WAS A CHILD.

THEY WOULD FORM A REAL SAGA OF YOUR LIFE.

ZELDA MAKES FRIENDS WITH A YOUNG ASPIRING WRITER IN MONTGOMERY, PAUL MCLENDON, WHO REGULARLY VISITS HER, BRINGING HER HIS SHORT STORIES. SHE GIVES HIM GOOD ADVICE.

AND IN MARCH 1947, A CERTAIN HENRY DAN PIPER, A GRADUATE OF PRINCETON, WHO HAS BEEN DISCHARGED FROM THE ARMY AN IS AN ADMIRER OF SCOTT, PAYS A VISIT.

I WANT T WRITE A BIOGRAPH OF SCOT

164

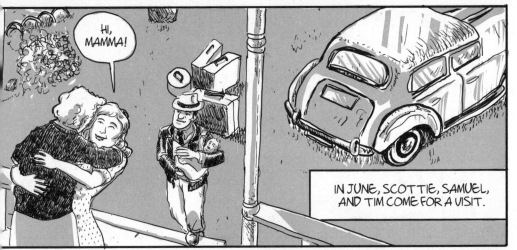

HI, MAMMA!

IN JUNE, SCOTTIE, SAMUEL, AND TIM COME FOR A VISIT.

ZELDA THROWS A PARTY FOR THEM, INVITING TWENTY GUESTS TO THE BLUE MOON RESTAURANT.

WE'RE GETTING OLD. IF WE WERE YOUNG WE'D RISE AND DANCE.

SOON AFTER, ZELDA HAS HER LAST RELAPSE. ON NOVEMBER 2, 1947, SHE GOES BACK TO HIGHLAND HOSPITAL.

MAMMA, DON'T WORRY. I'M NOT AFRAID TO DIE.

CAR SERVICE

165

ON MARCH 9, 1948, SHE WRITES TO SCOTTIE.

TO-DAY THERE IS PROMISE OF SPRING IN THE AIR AND AN AURA OF SUNSHINE OVER THE MOUNTAINS...

...THE MOUNTAINS SEEM TO HOLD MORE WEATHER THAN ELSEWHERE...

...AND TIME AND RETROSPECT FLOOD ROSEATE DOWN THE LONG HILL-SIDES.

IT WILL BE HER LAST LETTER.

166

EPILOGUE

THE DEATH OF ZELDA

ON MARCH 10, 1948, A FIRE BREAKS OUT IN THE KITCHEN OF THE MAIN WING OF HIGHLAND HOSPITAL.

THE FLAMES CLIMB TO THE ROOF AND SPREAD THROUGH EVERY FLOOR.

THE WOODEN FIRE ESCAPES BURN QUICKLY, AND THERE ARE NEITHER FIRE EXTINGUISHERS NOR IS THERE A SPRINKLER SYSTEM IN THE OLD BUILDING.

NINE WOMEN DIE IN THE FIRE, INCLUDING ZELDA.

HER BODY IS SO BADLY BURNED, SHE IS IDENTIFIED ONLY BY THE SLIPPER LYING BENEATH HER.

DEATH IS THE ONLY REAL ELEGANCE.

169

ON MARCH 17, ZELDA IS BURIED AT ROCKVILLE UNION CEMETARY.

FRANCIS SCOTT FITZGERALD

ZELDA SAYLE

IN THIS CEMETERY, BY SCOTT'S SIDE, ZELDA TOO WAS LAID TO REST, CONVEYED TO MARYLAND ON ST. PATRICK'S DAY, JOINING HIM EIGHT YEARS LATER, ON A WARM AND SUNNY DAY, AS SHARP A CONTRAST AS CAN BE IMAGINED TO THE STARK AND CHILLY DAY ON WHICH HER HUSBAND WAS INTERRED; THE FLOWERS THAT PEOPLE BROUGHT FOR HER WERE REALLY FOR THEM BOTH. AT LEAST THEIR MORTAL REMAINS, BENEATH THOSE FLOWERS, FINALLY FOUND PEACE.

FERNANDA PIVANO

BUT EVEN UNDER THOSE FLOWERS, THERE IS TO BE NO PEACE. IN 1975, THE ARCHDIOCESE OF WASHINGTON REVERSES ITS DECISION TO REFUSE SCOTT BURIAL IN A CATHOLIC CEMETERY...

...AND THE REMAINS OF THE FITZGERALDS ARE TRANSFERRED TO THE CEMETERY OF ST. MARY'S CHURCH.

FRANCIS SCOTT KEY
FITZGERALD
September 24. 1896
December 21. 1940
HIS WIFE
ZELDA SAYRE
July 24. 1900
March 10. 1948

ENGRAVED ON THE HEADSTONE ARE THE LAST WORDS OF THE GREAT GATSBY.

SO WE BEAT ON, BOATS AGAINST THE CURRENT, BORNE BACK CEASELESSLY INTO THE PAST.

THE GREAT GATSBY

BUT SOMEHOW I CAN'T FIND ANYTHING HOPELESS IN HAVING LIVED.

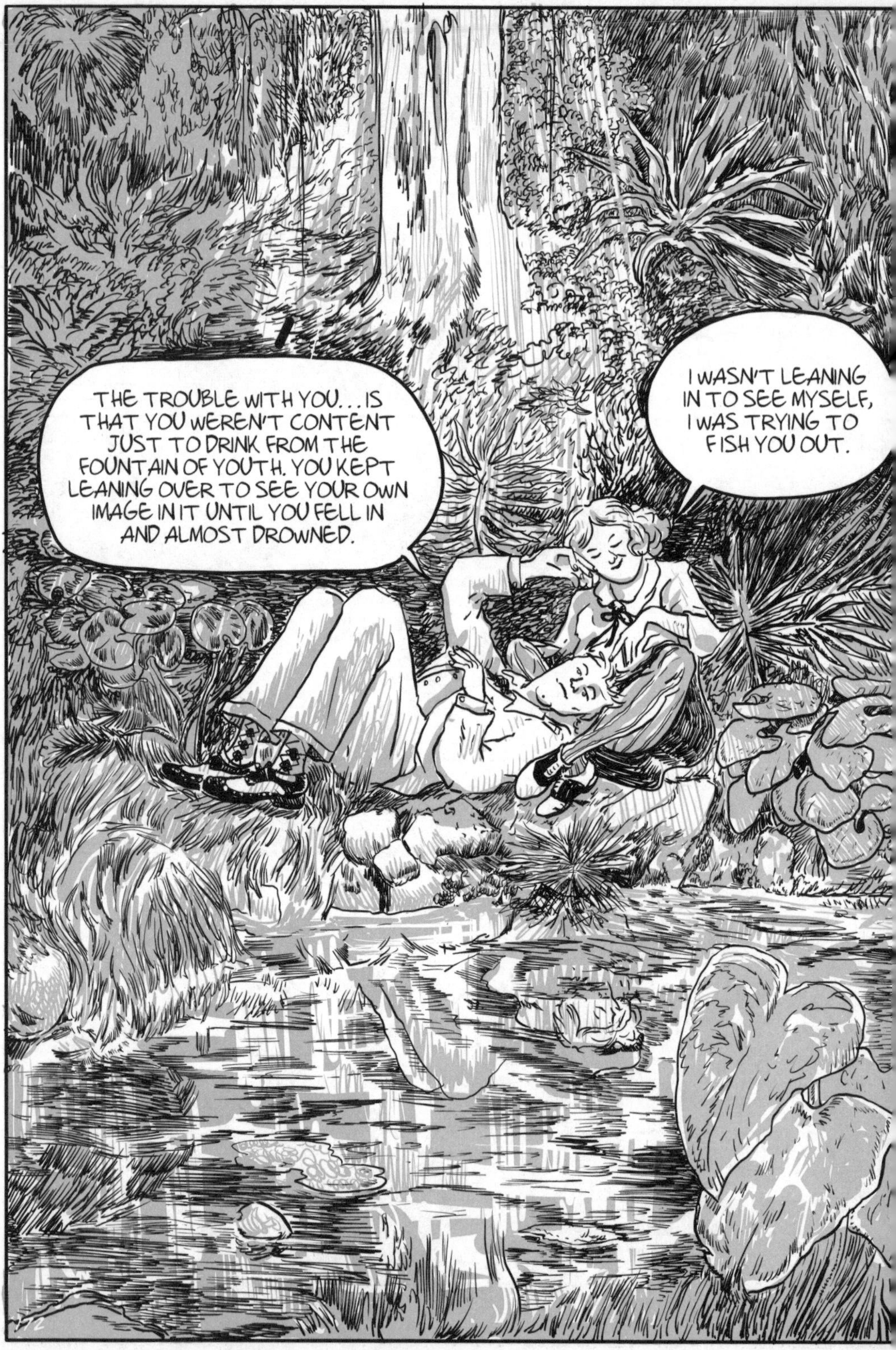
THE TROUBLE WITH YOU... IS THAT YOU WEREN'T CONTENT JUST TO DRINK FROM THE FOUNTAIN OF YOUTH. YOU KEPT LEANING OVER TO SEE YOUR OWN IMAGE IN IT UNTIL YOU FELL IN AND ALMOST DROWNED.
I WASN'T LEANING IN TO SEE MYSELF, I WAS TRYING TO FISH YOU OUT.

THE END

SOURCES

ALL OF THE NOVELS, STORIES, AND LETTERS OF SCOTT AND ZELDA FITZGERALD, THE BIOGRAPHIES OF BOTH OF THEM, AND ESPECIALLY *ZELDA*, BY NANCY MILFORD, AND *SCOTT FITZGERALD*, BY ANDREW TURNBULL; THE SCRAPBOOK *THE ROMANTIC EGOISTS*, EDITED BY MATTHEW J. BRUCCOLI, SCOTTIE FITZGERALD SMITH, AND JOAN P. KERR; ERNEST HEMINGWAY'S *A MOVEABLE FEAST*; AND BUDD SCHULBERG'S *THE DISENCHANTED*.

ACKNOWLEDGMENTS

I WISH TO THANK MY PARENTS FOR HAVING BROUGHT ME UP IN HOUSES FULL OF BOOKS, AND MY SISTER, ALESSIA, WHO NEVER STOPPED GIVING ME GIFTS OF SKETCHBOOKS. A THANK YOU GOES TO MAURIZIO BONO, AS WELL, FOR THE IDEA OF ILLUSTRATED REVIEWS, AND TO MICHAEL MUHAMMAD KNIGHT, WHO EXPLAINED THE MEANING OF ZELDA TO ME ONE DAY IN BALTIMORE.

I'D LIKE TO THANK MY PARENTS FOR ALWAYS HAVING PROVIDED ME WITH THE RIGHT TOOLS AND POINTING ME IN THE RIGHT DIRECTIONS. I THANK MARILENA ROSSI FOR STICKING BY ME, FOR ADVISING ME ON THE COSTUMES IN THE BOOK, AND FOR HELPING US BY DOING THE ORIGINAL SKETCHES OF THE CLOTHING WORN AT ZELDA'S WEDDING.

LAST AND LEAST TO MY WIFE, DAUGHTER, AUNTS, WHO PUT AT MY DISPOSAL LETTERS, WILLS, PORTRAITS, PHOTOGRAPHS, DOCUMENTS...

...STAMP BOOKS, POST-CARD COLLECTIONS, LAUNDRY MARKS, CIGAR BANDS, REPORT CARDS, DIPLOMAS, PARDONS, TRIALS, CONVICTIONS, ACCUSATIONS, LEASES AND UNPAID BILLS, STAMP COLLECTIONS AND CONFEDERATE MONEY.